Your River Must Flow!

How ANYONE May Minister the Anointing of the Holy Spirit

by

Albert Gengenbach

Fairmont Books is a ministry of The McDougal Foundation, Inc., a Maryland nonprofit corporation dedicated to spreading the Gospel of the Lord Jesus Christ to as many people as possible in the shortest time possible.

Published by:

𝒥airmont Books
P.O. Box 3595
Hagerstown, MD 21742-3595
www.mcdougalpublishing.com

ISBN 1-58158-030-4

Impreso en Colombia
Printed in Colombia

DEDICATION

This book is seven years long in living experience. Half of that time I spent in three countries in South America — Colombia, Argentina and Chile. During more than forty trips to those nations, I gave seminars on the material covered in this book. For a number of reasons, I made those trips by myself, leaving my wife, Peggy, home alone. Such a schedule was more than a little difficult for her. But more than that, our living and ministry expenses were never completely supplied by the offerings from the churches I served, and Peggy's work was important to our financial survival. I will always appreciate and be deeply grateful for the fact that her sacrifice enabled me to do the things the Lord was leading me to do in those years. I am conscious of the great price she paid at home alone. This book is dedicated to you, Peggy.

ACKNOWLEDGMENTS

I wish to acknowledge with warmest gratitude the heaven-sent aid supplied by three loving brothers who continually arranged for me to be received for ministry in churches where I was not known to the pastors. How grateful I am to them! They are Jorge Fresneda in Colombia, Hugo Castro in Argentina and Samuel Briceno, my pastor, in Bogota, Colombia.

CONTENTS

"If anyone is thirsty, let him come to me and drink. Whoever believes in me, as the Scripture has said, STREAMS [RIVERS, KJV] OF LIVING WATER will flow from within him." *By this he meant the Spirit.* John 7:37-39

INTRODUCTION

Evil is ever present in the world; there are spiritual beings that conspire to do wrong; there is a disorder in creation that often results in harm and destruction; and there are members of the human race who are born subject to an inner attraction to do evil. BUT the merciful, Almighty God has given the solution for these conditions. He has provided, through the Lord Jesus Christ, salvation from evil and its consequences for all men everywhere. Through our Lord Jesus Christ, God has provided for us the forgiveness of sins, the Word of God (the Bible) to lead and guide us, and the Holy Spirit whose power will dwell within us to counteract all evil forces at work and to strengthen us in our weaknesses.

The Church of the Lord Jesus Christ has rightly focused upon the need of mankind for repentance and forgiveness of sins. The study and teaching of the Scriptures has also been emphasized. But, although the Holy Spirit has been recognized as man's great source of help during his lifetime, the fact that the Spirit is present within *each* believer, ready to flow forth from him to do marvelous works of God whenever His power is desired or needed has gone unheralded. This is sad, for the Spirit of God is with us for a reason, to combat the forces of evil as they manifest themselves.

The anointing of the Spirit active within us is not to be a sporadic experience. As we will see, the Scriptures teach that each believer may have the anointing abiding within him permanently, and that it is God's will that this anointing flow out of us to bring about extraordinary blessings. God wants His children to live as overcomers of all evil — no matter what its source. Therefore, the Spirit must be active in us and through us.

There are some members of the Lord's Body who have learned these secrets and who periodically engage in a ministry of the anointing against evil forces and the harm they do. Because of this, these particular members have become famous. There remain, however, many millions of believers who have been enabled to do the same good work, but they have not yet realized it and, thus, have not taken up the fight. The result is that evil and its consequences are not being dealt with in the earth as they should be. The Church, as a whole, is not taking advantage of the full and wide salvation that has been provided for us.

The purpose of this book is to show that ALL BELIEVERS may benefit from the great power of the Spirit, the anointing, that is within them, and that all may minister the anointing! As we shall see, this is not a complicated matter, and the Lord Jesus has given us clear teaching on how this may be done. Anyone who follows His commands can minister the anointing and do all the things for which the power of the Holy Spirit is available to men. What could be more exciting?

Al Gengenbach
Upper Marlboro, Maryland

Part I

HOW to Minister the Anointing

CHAPTER 1

"IF ANYONE IS THIRSTY"

"If ANYONE is thirsty, let him come to me and drink. Whoever believes in me, as the Scripture has said, streams of living water will flow from within him." By this he meant the Spirit. John 7:37-39

"ANYONE"! The Lord begins His teaching on the Spirit by saying that the ministry of the Spirit, the ministry of the anointing, is for ANYONE! ANYONE may have the Holy Spirit to flow out from him or her to do works of divine power.

The Holy Spirit has always acted in power in the earth according to the sovereign will of God, and He does not require the agency of a human to activate His workings. In the first verses of the book of Genesis, we see the Holy Spirit already at work in creation — long before man's existence. On the Day of Pentecost, "suddenly," the Holy Spirit manifested Himself and worked wonders in Jerusalem. It was a sovereign act on His part. Later, with Saul on the road to Damascus, the Spirit initiated the supernatural encounter that began the dramatic change in that man's life.

However, the Holy Spirit also works in the earth as a result of what men do. Men may bring on His activity and His power by the things they do or do not do. God has chosen to allow men to be habitations of the Holy Spirit, and He then gives us the authority to loose the Spirit from within us to do signs and wonders. Thus, God has enabled us to become His agents for Holy Spirit power to work in the earth. This is nothing new. Men have been doing this all over the earth now for centuries. Through famous prophets like Moses, Elijah and Elisha,

11

through the disciples of Jesus like Peter, through learned men like Paul, and through humble people like the kitchen helper named Phillip, the Holy Spirit anointing has flowed with great power, and wondrous things have resulted.

This flowing forth of the Holy Spirit through men is what the Lord Jesus was talking about in John 7:37-39. He tells us that the power of the Spirit will be manifested, or will flow, through men. He also tells us who can do mighty works through the Holy Spirit and how they can be done. Right here we find the *who* and the *how* of the ministry of the anointing of the Holy Spirit.

Before I go any further, let me state plainly that I cannot speak for others. There are many well-known men who are powerful in this regard. They are well respected, and there is wonderful fruit from their ministries. Their service brings blessings to thousands of people. I have not consulted with such men on this subject, and I am not, therefore, speaking for them. In this book, I wish to center on the way, very plain and simple, that our Lord teaches us that ANYONE and EVERYONE can minister the anointing. In this way, the ninety-nine percent of the members of the Body of Christ who are not now ministering the anointing may begin to do so, and they may continue to do so all the days of their lives.

The infinite Spirit of God, with all of His divine power, is presently dwelling within millions of people in the earth. He has come into us to do things in us personally, but also to do things for others through us. This infinite power is not yet at work to any great degree through the majority of believers worldwide. The flow of the anointing is missing in and from the lives of far too many Christians, even those who have been baptized with the Holy Ghost. This is lamentable, for, according to the teaching of our Lord Jesus (and His teachings have been borne out by the experience of many), the person who is willing to do what He says in this short passage will discover that He will cause the anointing to flow out of him or her in power to accomplish great things, even to perform signs and wonders.

Christianity is weak, but God is not weak. Christianity is weak because of the lack of believers doing what Jesus declared that we should do. The world is starving, while God's barns are filled, because men and women are waiting to be touched by the power stored up in believers. The ministry of divine power through the anointing is available to us all, to ANYONE.

One of the reasons that so many Christians live without the power of the Holy Spirit flowing from them is the popular acceptance of the error that there are only a few people who have been constituted as agents to minister the anointing. It has been widely accepted that there are a certain few ministers in the world, or in any given local church, to whom others must go to receive the flow of the anointing and its accompanying blessings. It is unfortunate that some "recognized" ministers of the anointing perpetuate this error, enjoying the supposed exclusivity of their position. As new people are being saved and enter into church fellowship, only a few "super-spiritual" members are allowed to minister the anointing. The vast majority of Christians believe and live under this false understanding that there is some special calling from God to certain chosen leaders regarding the ministry of the anointing to do works of power.

It is true that there are certain people in the Body who are chosen and appointed to particular offices (see Ephesians 4:11 and 1 Corinthians 12:29-30). But the Lord plainly sets forth in these verses we are studying that there are no limits of personage regarding the anointing working in power through men and women. According to what He says in John 7:37-39, and contrary to what is widely accepted, we do not need the following things to minister the anointing:

- A special visitation from the Lord Jesus in which He constitutes a person as a minister of the anointing
- The attainment of a certain high level of spiritual maturity
- The attainment of a unique degree of personal holiness
- Hours spent continually in prayer and Bible reading
- Long periods of fasting to force the hand of God
- Having been a Christian for a long period of time
- Participation in seminary or Bible school studies

I am not speaking against any of these activities; I am simply saying that these things are not required for a person to be able to minister the anointing. ANYONE may do it. Because it is a common belief that many or all of these items are required in order to minister the anointing, the majority of Christians live without expressing Holy Spirit power in their lives. This is a tragic loss, not only to them, but also to others.

The Lord's words are simple and direct. They are about as concise as they could possibly be. Without any preamble or prerequisite, He has set forth a few simple things that, if done from the heart, will result in the flowing forth of the anointing from ANYONE to do powerful works. Jesus says that if we do these few things, the Holy Spirit will flow, and He is true to His word.

In this chapter of John, there is an account of the Lord attending the Feast of Tabernacles. This was the feast established in Old Testament times that prophetically spoke of the great and wide scope of the salvation that Messiah would bring to men. The feast foretold the great blessings that would flow among men, even as living water. The celebration of the feast looked to the day that Messiah, the Anointed One, would bring these blessings to men. It looked to the day that the Holy Spirit would freely express His power through and among men.

John tells us that on the last day of this feast Jesus was in the middle of a crowd of Jewish worshipers. He stood up and shouted out for all of them to hear that what they had been celebrating in anticipation during the past seven days of that feast was about to be realized through Him. *He* was the Anointed One (the Messiah) whom they and their forefathers had been awaiting for many centuries. He was the one who was to bring to them a rich and powerful salvation. He told them that these blessings would come through the gift of the Holy Spirit, who would flow out from men, from ANYONE, to bring blessings.

In verse 39, John made a clarification so that we could never misunderstand what Jesus was saying:

> *By this he meant the Spirit, whom those who believed in him were later to receive.*
> John 7:39

What beautiful words Jesus spoke that day! What a beautiful image

— living waters flowing from you and me! Waters, having life in themselves, bringing that life to men for needed blessings.

During the years that followed (and even up to our present day), these words have lifted the hearts of generations of Christians. This image has thrilled and edified believers for centuries. Believers have embraced it with joy and excitement and anticipation. I remember how these words stirred me deeply more than fifty-five years ago — though my understanding of them at the time was limited.

In the ensuing years, I have heard the words proclaimed loudly and with great emotion by many preachers and have seen the image they carry (flowing streams of living water) depicted on posters and calendars too many times to count. In several different countries, I have seen entire walls of churches painted with this image, flowing waters bringing refreshing. It is a comforting, uplifting and delightful image given to us by the Lord.

What a wonderful promise these words bring to us! Those who believe can be blessed; those who sorely need such blessings can receive.

There is just one thing that we, as believers, must do to receive these promises. We must take Jesus' words literally, in the great simplicity of their meaning. Because His words have not been believed and acted upon, we have not received the benefits He promised. If we have the Holy Spirit flowing in us, the many blessings of the Holy Spirit will become part of our lives.

Although this beautiful image presented by the Lord has captured the attention and the hearts of believers, we have been held back from receiving all that He promised because we have not taken His words as He intended them.

What Jesus told us here is a picture, a metaphor. It is given to us to help us understand a great spiritual reality, one that seems difficult for the human mind to grasp — the Spirit of God taking up permanent residence within a human being AND that infinite and divine Person coming forth from that human being to do things that would be refreshing to humanity! And this can happen whenever we wish it or need it! It is a mind-blowing concept! Because of this, the Lord gave us a simple material example of what this would somehow be like ... flowing streams of water that bring refreshing.

The great salvation our Lord was bringing to mankind was to be far more than forgiveness of sins (as necessary as that is to fallen mankind). The Lord was promising the restoration of man to permanent union with the Spirit of God, which had been lost to the race through the fall of Adam. Furthermore, He was revealing that man, having the Spirit of God dwelling within him, was now to take an active part in the flow of the Spirit from him for the demonstration of divine power in the earth. The divine life of God, by the Spirit, would be flowing actively from human temples that would be set up after He, the Lord Jesus, had been glorified.

Living waters! Waters that have life in themselves! Bringing refreshment to men! This was not to be natural water, which only aids and fosters life. These waters had life in themselves, for they are the very Spirit of God, the Spirit of life in Christ Jesus. And, again, this beautiful image of the Spirit of God flowing to men was to take place through men. What a wonder!

The sad thing is that men have focused on this beautiful image rather than on the person of the Holy Spirit and His desire to work through them. Men contemplate the image, and they celebrate it, but they do not go further to claim the spiritual reality for which it stands. For the most part, we have ceased to do the four simple things Jesus told us to do in order to bring forth the Holy Spirit with His power emanating from us.

If we will do four simple things, the Lord told us, then the anointing will flow in power from us. His divine life will flow from us to others to accomplish all the things for which the Spirit was sent.

Let us understand clearly this matter of the flowing living waters. This is only an image for our imaginations. It was given to help our understanding. There is no such thing in material or spiritual reality as "living waters." There is no actual flow of water of any kind.

The Lord was not talking here about water at all; He was promising the flow of His Spirit through a believer. He was saying that the Almighty Spirit of God can do wonderful works when He takes up residence in a man. He is revealing that the Holy Spirit will come to a man, not merely to settle down in him, but to become highly active in him and through him. He is explaining that the Spirit will give multiplied blessings, as the believer in whom He dwells does his part in the ministering of the anointing. He reveals here that the Spirit of God comes to a person to work blessings through him — such as only God can do.

This is the great and wide salvation the Lord Jesus came to give to mankind (see Hebrews 2:3). This is the wonderful Good News of the Gospel! This is the Gospel of Christ, the Anointed One, for all men who accept His terms for salvation. This is that which the Feast of Tabernacles looked forward to in Old Testament times (ever since the days of Moses). This is what the Lord Jesus was shouting loudly to proclaim that day.

THOSE WHO ARE TO MINISTER THE ANOINTING

Mark well the first thing the Lord Jesus says in these verses regarding the ministry of the Holy Spirit. Here He deals with *who* is able to minister the Spirit. This is important, and He tells us plainly:

- Who will have this permanent union with the Spirit of God
- Who will be the source in the earth of Spirit activity in power
- Whom God intends the Holy Spirit to act through
- Who will do signs and wonders by the Spirit
- Which chosen vessels will be thus honored, privileged and highly favored

And who is it? Jesus said, "ANYONE." He said that this great privilege of ministering the anointing in power was to be for any man, any woman, any child, any old person, any person whomsoever — ANYONE!

It might be profitable to consider again some of the things the Lord *did not say* about who could be a minister of the Spirit, for deeply rooted misunderstandings resist correction. We need to see and accept the fact that Jesus did not limit the ministry of the anointing to the relative few who have been active in it, both in the past and in the present time.

Jesus *did not* say that the ministry of the Spirit was only for an apostle, a Peter, for instance, or a Paul. He *did not* say that this ministry was to be for a few chosen people in any generation. He *did not* say that this ministry was to be only for those who attended seminary or Bible schools. He *did not* say that this ministry was to be only for certain uniquely prepared followers, whether we mean prepared by education, by spiritual maturity, or by having a been a believer for a good long time.

Jesus did not even say that this ministry would be only for renowned ministers, for those who are pastors of churches, or for those who sport some religious title — such as reverend, doctor, elder or deacon. He did not say that this ministry was limited to men, or that it was not for women. He also did not limit this ministry to adults. The Lord did not put any such limits on the ministry of the Spirit. It is His followers who have always done so.

The Lord Jesus said that this ministry of the anointing was for ANYONE, ANYONE who is willing to do what He has shown us in John 7:37-39. ANYONE can cause the anointing to flow from himself or herself with power.

ANYONE includes all those who are reading these words. You are an ANYONE. Personally, I have never met a person who did not qualify as an ANYONE. So, the Lord Jesus is addressing you. He is addressing me. He is addressing ANYONE and everyone with this awesome challenge. Every human being willing to hear Jesus' voice and obey can have the Spirit of God residing within, and every human being who is willing to hear Jesus' voice and obey can have the Spirit flowing forth in power from his or her life.

ANYONE can be active in this ministry of the Spirit — continually and daily. There are no limitations of age, sex, nationality or prior religious training. There are no limitations of earning power or profession.

God has created us in a most marvelous manner so that we have the capability of being indwelt by the divine. More than that, we have the privilege of causing the divine to proceed forth from ourselves to do powerful works. Every individual born into the world has this potential.

"If ANYONE Is Thirsty"

THE MYSTERY OF CHRIST

... Christ Jesus himself as the chief cornerstone. In him the whole building is joined together and rises to become a holy temple in the Lord. And in him you too are being built together to become a dwelling in which God lives by his Spirit.

For this reason I, Paul, the prisoner of Christ Jesus for the sake of you Gentiles — Surely you have heard about the administration of God's grace that was given to me for you, that is, the mystery made known to me by revelation, as I have already written briefly. In reading this, then, you will be able to understand my insight into the mystery of Christ, which was not made known to men in other generations as it has now been revealed by the Spirit to God's holy apostles and prophets. This mystery is that through the gospel the Gentiles are heirs together with Israel, members together of one body, and sharers together in the promise in Christ Jesus.

I became a servant of this gospel by the gift of God's grace given me through the working of his power. Although I am less than the least of all God's people, this grace was given me: to preach to the Gentiles the unsearchable riches of Christ, and to make plain to everyone the administration of this mystery, which for ages past was kept hidden in God, who created all things. His intent was that now, through the church, the manifold wisdom of God should be made known to the rulers and authorities in the heavenly realms, according to his eternal purpose which he accomplished in Christ Jesus our Lord.

Ephesians 2:20-3:11

In these verses, Paul deals with this great wonder: the Spirit of God indwelling men (see 2:22). He calls it *"the mystery of Christ"* (3:4). He says that this is *"the promise in Christ Jesus"* (3:6). And He says it is for all men — Jews and Gentiles.

"The mystery of Christ": This word *"Christ"* is from the Greek equivalent to the Hebrew word translated *"Messiah."* Both of these words mean the same — "the Anointed One." This was the great glory of the man Jesus: He was the Anointed One; the Holy Spirit was upon His life.

Jesus was the first man since Adam to have the Holy Spirit residing permanently in Him. The fact that this was even possible was *"hidden in God"* during the Old Testament days. Everything about the Holy Spirit taking up residence in man remained a mystery until the revelations that were given to Paul. As Paul uses this phrase, *"the mystery of Christ,"* this is what He is referring to. He is zeroing in on a particular aspect of the Lord, His anointing, as a man, with the Holy Spirit. And this is the great grace that has now been given to men, Paul shows, the same Spirit, the same anointing of the Holy Spirit. This has been given to the Church corporately, and to each believer individually. Paul's teaching in 1 Corinthians 3:16 shows this corporate indwelling of the Spirit, and 1 Corinthians 6:19 shows the individual indwelling.

There are, Paul shows here, unsearchable riches available to men, the *"unsearchable riches of Christ"* (Ephesians 3:8). Because we are in union with Christ, the Anointed One, we now have access to unsearchable riches through the ministry of this anointing which Christ has given us. These are the refreshings that come from the flowing of the living waters, the image the Lord has given us regarding the things that the anointing will produce when the Spirit comes forth from believers.

Paul knew his call from God. He was to proclaim and to explain this great gift of God to men, this *"mystery of Christ,"* heretofore hidden, but now revealed. It must be *"[made] plain to everyone"* (3:9). Everyone is to know how to minister this mystery of the anointing. Why? Because the Lord has said that this ministry is for ANYONE, and of course, that includes EVERYONE.

These are things that we must understand if the rivers of God's blessing are to flow all over the earth as He has declared they would. This Holy Spirit power has been given to us, and it is up to us to administer it.

We are touching on the eternal purpose of God for each human being. He desires that each man and woman be filled with His Spirit and that the anointing of the Spirit be activated with power through us as we live daily in the earth.

Adam lost this touch on his life, and he lost it for his descendants. Jesus, however, paid the price, that we might be redeemed back into this relationship. In our age, we have not yet experienced what the anointing will do in the fullness of its expression, but we most certainly have *"the deposit"* (Ephesians 1:14) of the Spirit — the guarantee of the fullness to come.

The Spirit was sent to the earth to do many specific works, and God intends for rivers of blessings to flow from us now, not mere trickles. His idea was for EVERYONE to be ministering the flow of the anointing.

This is salvation's great purpose — man restored to intimate union with God! God dwelling within man! God and man together, working out His eternal plan in His creation! This is the restoration of the race to the position Adam lost for us — administrators of the divine power of the Holy Spirit, ever in submission to Him who indwells us.

This is the great glory of the man Jesus, the Christ, the Anointed One, through whom ANYONE and EVERYONE can now have the anointing of the Spirit in them and active through them. This is the great *"promise in Christ Jesus"* in which we ALL share, this great glory of the Anointed One!

How awesome this great calling to man, yet in his fallen, naturally unholy state! Awesome, but very real, as the Spirit made clear, speaking through Paul:

> *Now to him who is able to do immeasurably more than all we ask or imagine, according to his power that is at work within us, to him be glory in the church and in Christ Jesus throughout all generations, for ever and ever! Amen.*
>
> Ephesians 3:20-21

We cannot say it too much. The ministry of the Spirit is for ANYONE, and thus for EVERYONE.

I am reminded of a comment I read years ago by the famous Mahatma Gandhi. He once said, "Christianity is an interesting religion. Its claims are highly noble and sublime. What a pity that it has never been tried."

What a pity indeed! We are all called to minister the anointing to do the things for which Jesus sent the Spirit into the world. There are no special individuals constituted by the Lord Jesus as the only ministers of the anointing. The Bible does record the story of men and women who were uniquely called to particular ministries or services, people like Peter and Paul. But the Scriptures also record the great signs and wonders worked by the Spirit through humble men like Phillip, a kitchen worker, a waiter on tables.

A COMMON STUMBLING BLOCK

One of the most common stumbling blocks that hinders many from ministering the anointing is the question of whether or not they are worthy to do so. In this ministry of the Spirit, however, worthiness or unworthiness is not a consideration (just as being holy enough or prepared enough are also not factors). No one can rightly plead such personal lacks as a legitimate reason to refrain from ministering the Holy Spirit. The reason is that no one is worthy for such ministry. Every man and every woman is unworthy — both of having the Holy Spirit live within them and of being agents for His ministrations. There is none who can claim to be worthy to minister the Holy Spirit.

But this is not a problem. This is exactly where the Lord starts — with unworthy mankind. He knows our unworthiness far better than we do, and yet He has said that ANYONE can minister the Spirit by doing as He says. So, that's settled, and it is time for every one of us to get on with obeying God! It is time for all of us to become active in the ministry of the anointing! It is time for us to accept the truth of God's Word on this matter. He has chosen us, knowing that we are unworthy vessels, to be the containers of the Holy Spirit.

When you come right down to it, who else did God have? Could He find perfect people to do His work? All men are fallen and weak. If God can't use us, whom can He use?

In spite of the unholiness of our flesh and our human weaknesses, however, God has decided that we are to have the Holy Spirit living within us. We are to show forth His glory, the anointing upon us and moving through us. Thus, God has chosen that ANYONE and EVERYONE can minister the Holy Spirit. This means you and it means me. So, let's get busy — all of us!

Paul declared that the mystery of Christ, the anointing and its activity in and through men, had been hidden in times past, but that it was now revealed. Why is this still a mystery to us? The Spirit indwelling

22

us, the Spirit flowing from us to others! This can no longer remain hidden. We may not understand it totally, but we can act upon it nevertheless.

> *I have become its [the Body of Christ's] servant by the commission God gave me to present to you the word of God in its fullness — the mystery that has been kept hidden for ages and generations, but is now disclosed to the saints. To them God has chosen to make known among the Gentiles the glorious riches of this mystery, which is Christ [the Anointed One] in you, the hope of glory. We proclaim him, admonishing and teaching everyone with all wisdom, so that we may present everyone perfect in Christ [the Anointed One]. To this end I labor, struggling with all his energy, which so powerfully works in me.* Colossians 1:25-29

Christ, the Anointed One, is in human beings with the Holy Spirit, poised to flow forth, revealing the glory of God. Paul lived to proclaim this mystery and to teach it, to explain it to everyone he met. His idea of being perfectly in union and harmony with Christ (the Anointed One) was that the anointing in the believer was being expressed in the life of that believer, and was being expressed through him to others. EVERYONE ministering the anointing! Always! Everywhere! EVERYONE expressing the glory of God!

And so, unworthy as we are, every single one of us, to minister the glorious anointing, this ministry is given to us all as a calling from our Lord. Let us stop stumbling over our admitted unworthiness. Let us cease to analyze and wonder: *How can this be possible for me?* Let us not get bogged down in anything that would hinder us from taking the place to which the Anointed One has called us.

True humility will say, "I am not worthy, Lord, but I will obey You. I will give myself to the ministry of the anointing You have given to EVERYONE, including me! I will do my part in the showing forth of the glory of God to others. I am willing to take to my heart the four simple things you tell us to do in John 7:37-39. I will meditate on them, and I will obey them." Any other attitude is foolish pride, and as marvelous and unthinkable as it may seem to us, EVERYONE who does this will find himself or herself ministering the anointing of the Spirit in power and glory.

So, let us hear what our Master is telling us to do. Let us believe the straightforward words He speaks to us. Let us determine to do the simple things He asks of us. Let each of us take seriously the privileged position to which He has called us: minister of the anointing. Each of us lives in a unique place, where he or she meets unique circumstances and unique people whom others never meet, and thus we are each presented with unique opportunities in life to minister God's blessings to others. His desire is that each of us, in our own unique circle of life, be a continuing source of the flow of the Spirit, that each of us be a hearer and a doer of John 7:37-39, that each of us be an active minister of the anointing.

This is the Lord's idea of what a real Christian should be in the world — a person filled with His Spirit who is pouring out to others. Are you among these ANYONEs, these EVERYONEs of whom the Lord is speaking? Ask yourself this question: Do you have the baptism of the Holy Spirit? If you do, then you have been ordained by the Lord Jesus to minister the anointing. You have been equipped and empowered and strategically placed in your community to minister the anointing to others in power. You are called to bring Holy Spirit blessings to others according to their needs.

It may sound strange to you, but say these words to yourself; speak them out loud: "I have been ordained by the Lord Jesus as a minister of the Holy Spirit!" Say it boldly. Speak this truth out until you become accustomed to its reality. This is the truth of the Word of God in your regard. Begin to believe this truth about yourself, and then begin to act it out, and keep acting it out continually. Live it — always.

If you have not, as yet, received the baptism of the Holy Spirit, seek to receive this anointing by inquiring among those who already have it. The Lord Jesus is waiting to give it to you. He has said that it is for ANYONE!

CHAPTER 2

"IF ANYONE IS THIRSTY"

"If anyone is THIRSTY, let him come to me and drink. Whoever believes in me, as the Scripture has said, streams of living water will flow from within him." By this he meant the Spirit.   John 7:37-39

For ANYONE desiring to minister the Spirit, four things are required:

1. He is to be thirsty.
2. He is to come to Christ.
3. He is to drink.
4. He is to believe in Christ.

Do these, the Lord says, and the anointing will flow from you to do wonderful things.

What did Jesus mean by this first requirement, that we must be thirsty? We human beings have been created with a faculty to desire. What we behold or contemplate we can desire, or long after, and such a desire can become a strong longing. A great thirst can develop in us when we do not have what we want.

Desires, of course, can be good and bad. There are a number of things that the Scriptures tell us we should thirst for. God wants us to have good desires, good thirsts. For example:

- We are to thirst after righteousness. (Matthew 5:6)
- We are to thirst after the Lord Jesus personally. (Psalm 42:1-2, 63:1 and Song of Solomon 1:1-3)

25

- We are to thirst after wisdom and understanding. (Psalm 19:8)
- We are to thirst after a love for the Word of God. We should cherish it and seek after it. (Psalm 119:72 and 97)
- We are to thirst after holy things. (Psalm 20:4)
- We are to thirst to do good. (Psalm 40:8)
- We are to thirst for what is good. (Romans 7:18)
- We are to thirst for greater spiritual gifts. (1 Corinthians 12:31)
- We are to thirst for a holy life. (Hebrews 13:18)
- We are to thirst for the things God desires. (3 John 2)

What exactly is the Lord telling us to be thirsty for in John 7:37-39? What is it that can cause the anointing to flow from us? To find the answer to that question, let us again examine the image the Lord has given us in John 7:37-39.

Here the Lord speaks of flowing streams which will bring refreshment to those in need of water. Men need water in order to live and function. When there is a lack of a proper water source, men begin to seek for one. They must have it. They can't live without it.

The longer our bodies go without water, the more thirsty we feel. If we can't find it, we will begin to function poorly, and eventually, we will die. The water in our bodies must be replenished. It is a matter of life and death.

This was a natural picture that the Lord Jesus gave us to help us understand what He was saying about the Holy Spirit and why He was given to us. The Spirit is present in us so that we might supply a needed provision that will refresh those around us. Living creatures have this requirement, regardless of their circumstances in life. When a water source is threatened, life itself is hangs in a delicate balance.

Men and women around us have needs. They are burdened and oppressed. They need provision in every area of their lives — physical, material, economic, spiritual, social, career-wise, etc. When such needs or burdens present themselves, men naturally begin to develop a desire for whatever is lacking in their lives. They begin to thirst after the thing they need. And they remain thirsty until they have received it.

The Lord is saying that the Holy Spirit will act to bring provisions and blessings to men when they are faced with lack or need in their lives. They will be refreshed as Holy Spirit supply comes to them through us. The Holy Spirit will be to them even as water, to give them supply and refreshings, according to their needs.

A given person, then, may be facing a particular need or lack in some area of his life and be without the supply he must have to continue living. He then begins to desire, or be thirsty for, that thing. He wants it, and he wants it more each passing moment. A person who has the Holy Spirit living within him may minister the Spirit to this needy individual, or cause the anointing to flow to him, in order that the supply that is lacking be provided through the power of the Holy Spirit.

In John 7:37, however, the Lord is saying that the person who desires to minister to the spiritual needs of others must first thirst himself. If the one doing the ministering has all the provision he wants at the moment for himself, then he is to thirst, to desire a supply, on behalf of the others who are lacking it. In this way, the one ministering the anointing enters into the thirst of those who are needing it.

Thirst, then, in this context, refers to being deeply and personally involved in the matter at hand. For us, it cannot be considered a minor or insignificant thing. It is a necessity, something that we must have. Someone has a need for this supply, and that need has now become serious. This is a deep matter, even an emotional one, one that will not go away or be satisfied with something less than what is needed. The Lord is telling us that the person who would minister the anointing must get involved personally in the matter for which he is ministering. This ministering is not to be a matter of impersonal service. This is not a service free of feeling. The one who ministers the anointing must identify personally with the longing, the thirst, of the one to whom he is ministering.

The Lord is telling us to pour ourselves out on behalf of the needs of others. We must feel their lack and their thirst and want it for them as much as they want it for themselves.

It is important that we realize God's desire in all of this. He wills to give needed provisions to men in their daily living. If one is not convinced that it is God's will to give such supply, he will frequently be blocked from acquiring a deep thirst for it in the Spirit.

God has created man as a dependent creature. He is dependent for his daily necessities on provisions and supply that God built into His creation surrounding man. All men depend for their provisions in life on something to be supplied from outside themselves; they depend, for needed provision, on other people or on situations often outside their own control. They depend on physical and material forces, such as the force of gravity and benevolent atmospheric conditions, for these affect the production of the food on which man depends. Men, therefore, need other men, and they need favorable circumstances in order to survive. This great dependency is built into man's nature by his Creator.

It is even more true in the spiritual sense. Whether or not men accept it, they are totally dependent upon God's Spirit for life. The profound revelation of the first chapter of Ezekiel testifies to this. In the New Testament, Paul asserted (in Acts 17:28) that only in union with God does a man even continue to exist (*"live"*), make any move at all, or even *"have his being."* God made man a very dependent creature.

God created man to live in continual dependence upon Him as his ultimate Supplier of all the provisions needed in life. (See Psalm 23 and 91, Proverbs 3:5-6, Isaiah 31:1, Matthew 11:28-29 and John 15:4 as examples of the many scriptural teachings on this point.)

In the beginning, when God created man, He declared that what He had done was *"good."* This was true of everything God created. There was an ample supply and provision for all, and the flow of needed blessings was in no way impeded. All this was due to the infinite goodness, wisdom, planning and power of the infinitely wonderful and good Creator. But the stark reality for men living today in this present world is that they still have the same requirements for life, but the provisions to meet their needs does not always come to them readily when they need it. Furthermore, burdens, difficulties and oppressions are rife in the earth. The forces in nature, circumstances, situations and people seem to conspire against us to cause us profound need, and the answer to that need is often not naturally available to us.

What has happened? There has occurred a great disruption in the functioning of the creation as God initially fashioned it. As a result of the rebellion of Adam against his Creator, the spirit world and the material world no longer work in their initially created harmony. The consequences of the sin of Adam have been destructive to the good working order of things that the good Creator built into His handiwork. Now, material and spiritual forces (including evil spirit beings) are at work against man, wishing him harm and destruction. These continually deprive men of an ample supply and of the freely flowing provisions the Creator always intended men to have. This is the bad news of the state of man in creation.

However, there is good news as well, and the good news is that the infinitely good Creator still desires blessings and ample provision for men, as they require them. He has provided, in Christ, both restoration to His good graces and also the Holy Spirit to indwell His people. By means of this indwelling anointing, He now works to deter and to destroy the works and forces of evil. By this same anointing, He will also give to men the blessings and provisions they need for living out the will of their Creator in their daily lives.

God wills that men have blessings and that their needs be supplied. The Holy Spirit has said this clearly through the words of John:

> *Beloved, I wish above all things that thou mayest prosper and be in health, even as thy soul prospereth.*　　　　　3 John 2, KJV

Centuries before the coming of the Messiah (the Anointed One, who has also given the anointing to us), God revealed His will, that when the anointing would be given to men, it would be for the lifting of their burdens, and the destruction of oppressions in their lives. Isaiah foretold it:

> *And it shall come to pass in that day, that his burden shall be taken away from off thy shoulder, and his yoke from off thy neck, and the yoke shall be destroyed because of the anointing.*　　　　　Isaiah 10:27, KJV

God's will is to deliver men from evil and to give them the blessings and ample supply needed in life — spiritually, physically, materially, psychologically and economically. Our Creator has always desired fullness for His beloved human creatures — body, soul and spirit. For this, the Lord Jesus came to earth. He said He had come to bring *"life"* in all its aspects, and that He desired for men to have it *"more abun-dantly"* (John 10:10, KJV).

Jesus provided us with forgiveness for our sins, and this opened to us the door to all the good things He desired for us. Then, His way of continuing to give us an abundant supply was by restoring the Holy Spirit to us. With the anointing of the Holy Spirit permanently in a man, God's divinity is present to supply him with all that he needs and with power to thwart the workings of spirit enemies and their forces.

THE GOSPEL OF CHRIST

God has ordained that burdens and oppressions should not prevail against us or defeat us. This is the good news God has for all men to-day. This is *"the gospel of Christ"* (the Anointed One).

What exactly do the Scriptures mean by *"the gospel of Christ"*? More than eighty times in the New Testament, this word *"gospel"* appears — alone and without any other word or words to modify it. As such, it speaks of the good news that the Lord Jesus brought to mankind from the Father, good news that is both very deep and very broad.

There are many other times that the word "gospel" appears in the Scriptures with modifying words that point to certain aspects of that good news to men. Specific portions of that good news are pointed to, often within the context of which the writer is dealing. For example, the Bible speaks of *"the gospel of God's grace"* (Acts 20:24), *"the gospel of the kingdom"* (Matthew 4:23 and 9:35, KJV), *"the gospel of salvation"* (Ephesians 1:13), *"the gospel of peace"* (Romans 10:15, KJV) and *"the ev-erlasting gospel"* (Revelation 14:6, KJV).

There are many places in the Bible where the message from God to man is referred to specifically as *"the gospel of Christ."* Paul refers to it in this way (Romans 1:16, 15:19 and 29, 1 Corinthians 9:12 and 18, 2 Corinthians 4:4, 9:13 and 10:14, Galatians 1:7, Philippians 1:27 and 1 Thessalonians 3:2, KJV). To what aspect of the great and broad good news does He refer by this expression?

"If Anyone Is THIRSTY"

By using the word *"Christ"* here, Paul is clearly focusing on a particular aspect of the Lord Jesus, and that is His anointing. He is referring, therefore, to the gospel, or good news, brought by the Anointed One, or to the good news as regards the anointing of the Holy Spirit that was upon the man Jesus.

Jesus of Nazareth was born into the world as a man. He lived His life on earth as a man, subject to all human limitations, but without sin (see Philippians 2:6-8.) He was born and grew to manhood, but the Holy Spirit had not yet come upon Him to do works of power. Then, when He was at the age of thirty, the anointing of the Holy Spirit came to Him. That day, He became the Christ, the Anointed One, the Messiah. He was still a human being, but the anointing of the Spirit was permanently with Him.

For the last three and a half years of His life in ministry, Jesus was a living demonstration of how the Holy Spirit should act in and through a man:

> *God anointed Jesus of Nazareth with the Holy Spirit and with power, who went about doing good and healing all who were oppressed by the devil, for God was with Him.*   Acts 10:38, NKJ

Before He left the earth again, Jesus told us that the same things the Holy Spirit had done through Him would be done through us — and even greater works than these (see John 14:12). He said that it was good for us that He would leave the earth, for then He would send the Holy Spirit to dwell in each of us with power, just as the Spirit had been in Him to do the good works He had been doing (see John 16:7). A major part of the good news He brought to men was the revelation that His followers would have the anointing in them, just as he had it in Him. This anointing, He said, would come upon them to do Holy Spirit works, even as it had come upon Him.

In this way, the prophecy of Isaiah 10:27 would be fulfilled. The anointing came to the Messiah, the Christ, and then, through Him, it was to come to all men who receive Him as Lord and Savior and are baptized in the Holy Spirit.

THE ANOINTING IS THE HOLY SPIRIT

There is no anointing apart from the Holy Spirit. He is the anointing. It is not merely a feeling, as some believe. It is the divine person of the Holy Spirit:

You have an anointing from the Holy One.
The anointing you received from him remains in you.

1 John 2:20 and 27

Certainly, the anointing of the Holy Spirit may be sensed, or felt. Those in whom the Holy Spirit has come to dwell in power often sense His presence; they feel Him. But there are times that the Spirit's presence is not felt, and that doesn't mean that He has withdrawn His presence. These two promises are that once the anointing comes into a person, it stays with him permanently — whether he is aware of it or not.

When verse 27 tells us that the anointing remains, it means that the Holy Spirit remains. The anointing is the Holy Spirit; they are one and the same. And whether His presence is being manifested or not, He remains with us and in us. The Holy Spirit, or the anointing, remains in one who is baptized with the Spirit permanently to do the many matters that the Lord sent Him to do in us and through us. He is always present in us to give provision and supply for the needs of ourselves and others — body, soul and spirit.

Since the anointing is always with us, it may always be ministered by the one in whom the Spirit dwells. Holy Spirit power activity is available to ANYONE and EVERYONE, EVERYWHERE and ANYTIME! This is *"the gospel of Christ"*! This is the good news about Him. Jesus had this wonderful anointing with power, and He has given it to us.

This was the great glory of the man Jesus, the anointing upon Him with power! He was ever doing things that men and women around Him greatly needed. And, to the great glory of His grace, He has given us that same anointing with power to do the same works He did. This, again, is *"the glorious gospel of Christ"*:

32

"If Anyone Is THIRSTY"

The god of this world hath blinded the minds of them which believe not, lest the light of THE GLORIOUS GOSPEL OF CHRIST, who is the image of God, should shine unto them.   2 Corinthians 4:4, KJV

God wills to give blessings to men. He wills to destroy burdens and oppressions that come to them. And He desires to work through us.

There is great need these days to guard against a religiosity that exists among many of those who call themselves Christians. Far too many hold the view that God does not now work with His supernatural power to give material and/or natural benefits to men. Those who believe thus hold that the works done by the Holy Spirit through the Lord Jesus when He was on earth will no longer be done through men today. They believe that God is interested in dealing with only spiritual things today, but exactly the contrary is true.

God created this immense material world in all its fine microscopic detail and its vast macroscopic scope and workings. In this material creation, He set to work many intricate and inter-involved powers and forces. Indeed, all His complicated workings in the material creation greatly transcend human knowing and understanding. Obviously, His interest in material matters is far beyond great.

As I noted earlier, in the first chapter of the book of Ezekiel there is a profound revelation regarding the keen interest of God in His physical creation and His present active involvement with it. There we are shown the three persons of the Trinity busily at work in the multitude of functionings in nature.

God's present activity in creation is set forth there in symbolic, or picture, form in a complex vision that He gave to Ezekiel. For many years, I had no clue as to what this vision meant. Its meaning finally became clear to me as I studied some commentaries on the subject. As a result, I now have an ever-deepening and ever-growing appreciation of God's continual involvement in the workings of creation. Of special value, regarding the ministry of the anointing, is the impacting revelation in this chapter of the great activity of the Holy Spirit in all the functionings of the material world.

The revelation given to Ezekiel keeps giving me more and more appreciation and understanding of Paul's words:

Your River Must Flow!

He [God] is not far from each one of us. "For in him we live and move and have our being."   Acts 17:27-28

Truly, it is a great error to believe that God is interested in and now working with *only* spiritual matters and spiritual blessings. This error is contrary to many portions of the Scriptures. Furthermore, such that hold to this error do so to their own great personal loss. Also, their view results in detraction from the grand scope of the glory of God in His many material workings. Consider how many millions of men remain unconverted because Christians have not taken their God-intended places as active agents to impact others with the realities of God's power.

There is a need for fuller understanding of what the Word of God teaches regarding the wide scope of *"the gospel of Christ."* The Gospel of God does proclaim pardon to men for their sins and a blessed life in the ages to come, but included in the great Good News from God is *"the gospel of Christ."* Again, this word "Christ" specifically points to the anointing of the Holy Spirit on the Lord Jesus—the same Holy Spirit anointing He has made available to His followers. By the anointing we have, there has been given to us Holy Spirit power for wonderful provision of supernatural protection against burdens and oppressions. There are available natural blessings of many sorts now in this present life. So many of them are waiting in the Spirit for the taking through the ministry of the anointing.

To those who have not seen this in the past, and to those who have not taken advantage of it fully, it is time to broadcast everywhere *"the gospel of Christ."* It is time for all to learn the principles of John 7:37-39 and for them to be practiced and demonstrated everywhere.

New believers should be taught to enter into the blessings that come from their ministering of the anointing. They should be taught this immediately upon conversion. The ministry of the anointing should become a regular and essential part of normal Christian living. Upon hearing and learning how ANYONE can put to use the simple steps the Lord Jesus gives us regarding how to minister the anointing, it is for all to respond with ministry activity.

Remember, God has fashioned us as dependent beings who thirst

34

after needed supply, and it is His will to provide those things for which we thirst.

We must bring this thirst to the ministry of the anointing. He will be faithful to His promises in John 7:37-39. The anointing will flow as He has said it would. The Holy Spirit will give the supply.

Let's go a bit further. We have now established that a minister of the anointing is to thirst after the blessing needed, that the Lord Jesus has given him the anointing, to remain in him permanently, and that the anointing will flow through him to accomplish what is required in the one who has a need.

When I come to minister the anointing to others for what they need, the Lord would have me remember how much I thirst for my own provision when I am, myself, in need. So, when I am ministering the Spirit to others for their supply, I get involved and thirst on their behalf. I become thirsty for the same thing they are thirsty for, and I desire it just as I would if I needed it myself. We are to have hearts that are capable of feeling the needs of those to whom we minister and of bearing their burdens.

For example, we are to have a sincere desire that a sick person be healed. We are to have a yearning that a burden be lifted from one who is oppressed. We are to feel a thirst for a blessing that another person needs. If there is no urgency in us about the need, we may not be effective in ministering to that person. The one ministering must be urgent before the Lord for the result he or she is seeking on behalf of another.

The ministry of the anointing, then, is to be exercised with heartfelt emotion, with compassion, with love. There is to be an intensity in the person ministering on behalf of the one receiving. The Lord Jesus was our example, and He clearly felt the needs of those around Him. He clearly thirsted to supply the needs of others. He ministered with COMPASSION:

But when He saw the multitudes, he was MOVED WITH COMPASSION for them.   Matthew 9:36, NKJ

They said to Him, "Lord, that our eyes may be opened." So Jesus HAD COMPASSION, and touched their eyes. And immediately their eyes received sight, and they followed Him.   Matthew 20:33-34, NKJ

A man with leprosy came to him and begged him on his knees, "If you are willing, you can make me clean."
FILLED WITH COMPASSION, Jesus reached out his hand and touched the man. "I am willing," he said. "Be clean!" Immediately the leprosy left him and he was cured.   Mark 1:40-41

When Jesus saw the hungry multitude, He said:

I have COMPASSION for these people; they have already been with me three days and have nothing to eat.   Mark 8:2

Then He proceeded to work a great miracle to supply food for them.

Jesus was moved when He saw a mother weeping for her only son who had died. He stopped and raised the child to life again (see Luke 7:12-15).

When the Lord tells us to thirst as we minister the anointing, He is simply saying to do as He did when He ministered to others. This works for any need — for burdens that need to be lifted, for oppressions that need to be destroyed, for deliverance or financial blessing.

Our Lord ministered in faith and with love, and Paul learned to do likewise. He spoke to the Galatians of *"faith, which works by love"* (Galatians 5:6).

THE EXAMPLE OF A.A. ALLEN

I am often reminded of the great example of Evangelist A.A. Allen. Some forty-five years ago, he was one of the better-known ministers of the anointing. When he came to conduct a series of tent meetings in the Washington, D.C., area, a close friend of mine was in attendance one night. This friend was able to be close to the front where the ministry was taking place and was able to closely observe how Brother Allen ministered. He later told me this story:

A woman came forward holding her young child in her arms. The arms of the child were held pressed close to its chest. As my friend looked more closely, he realized that the child's arms were undeveloped. There were no defined hands. The arms and hands (such as they were) were atrophied and remained motionless at the chest. They appeared to my friend to be very much like the wings of a plucked chicken, plastered to its breast and ready for roasting. It was not funny; it was a pitiful and tragic sight!

Brother Allen took the child from his mother's arms and clasped it to his breast, saying not a word at first. He closed his eyes, as he began to communicate with the Lord. Gradually, he began to weep. Then, he started to sob, and tears streamed down his cheeks.

Still, he had not spoken a single word, and he remained this way for about ten minutes. It was obvious to everyone that he was feeling heart-wrenching compassion and love for this child and this mother. He longed deeply for the child's healing.

Then, as my friend watched, Brother Allen opened his arms and tenderly returned the child to his mother. Both arms were now perfectly formed, both hands and fingers perfectly defined!

Brother Allen knew how to minister the anointing! He genuinely thirsted after the supply that was needed at the moment, and consequently, he poured himself into the ministry on behalf of the one he was serving.

I think of this example when I am about to minister the anointing to others. Although I have not yet been able to acquire that same level of sensitivity, the example helps me to remember what the Lord says ministry of the anointing requires. This is especially helpful to me in cases of people in dire physical conditions, for instance, those with ugly malformations. In these cases, our initial human response is: "Oh, Lord, such a hard case!" But this human thinking must be replaced with genuine compassion and love — if we are to see the Spirit do His work.

AN OLD TESTAMENT PROMISE

I have dedicated Chapter 6 of this book to the subject "As the Scripture Has Said," and that portion deals with the promises of Ezekiel 47:1-12. What I learn there helps me to be reassured regarding the will of God to heal — to give life and to give it more abundantly through the flowing of the anointing.

In this vision, Ezekiel was shown the future Holy Spirit temples which we have now become. Their great function would be that the Spirit would come forth from them to bring great blessings in the earth continually.

The book of Acts shows the anointing beginning to flow from such human temples, just as the prophet saw. Today, there are many millions of such anointed temples scattered throughout every part of the earth. The will of God is that the Spirit flow in power from each and every temple.

The vision was given to Ezekiel many centuries ago, but it can only be realized as each temple does what is required in its own particular living situation and experience.

The Lack of Thirst

At times, when I am ministering the anointing, I have no difficulty getting personally involved on behalf of those who are seeking to receive from the Lord (being physically and mentally rested before a service helps me a lot in this regard). Sometimes the thirst comes readily, and is strong. At other times, however, there does not seem to be any thirst present at all. Then, I also experience varying degrees of thirst between these two extremes.

The difference does not seem to be where I am at the time. I minister the anointing in scheduled meetings in churches and to groups who meet in other places. But I also minister the anointing anywhere and everywhere — wherever the need presents itself and where people are open to receive from God. Therefore, I am continually confronted with enemies to my personal thirst on behalf of others' needs. Some of these enemies are my own personal interests at any given time and place, my personal concerns and my personal weaknesses. All these and more work against my ability to express genuine compassion and thirst on behalf of another.

The word of the Lord to me is clear to me: "Al, thirst and the anointing will flow. Get involved personally, on behalf of the person(s) standing before you." Therefore, when genuine thirst is lacking or seems limited, I begin to discipline myself to receive it. I look to the Lord in dependence on Him for His compassion. I abide in Him for what I need but lack at that time. I express faith in the reality that the love of God has been poured forth in my heart by the Spirit He has given me (see Romans 5:5). The Spirit of love and of compassion is within me — whether or not I am sensing it at a given moment. The life of the True Vine is ever flowing to me, and I receive it in faith and expectation.

With this faith for the compassion of the Lord Jesus to flow through me, I proceed into the period of ministry. Soon, the former apathetic feelings ebb, and sensings of thirsting and compassion begin to arise in me. The anointing begins to come upon me and to flow to those who are in need.

CHAPTER 3

"LET HIM COME TO ME"

"If anyone is thirsty, LET HIM COME TO ME and drink. Whoever believes in me, as the Scripture has said, streams of living water will flow from within him." By this he meant the Spirit. John 7:37-39

Jesus, the Christ, the Anointed One, is the expert on the anointing, and He tells us what a person, any person, is to do, in order that the Holy Spirit may proceed out from him to give blessings: *"Let him come to Me."* He is to focus on the Lord Jesus.

What did Jesus mean when He said, "Come to Me"? He was not requiring that we hop on a spiritual spacecraft to visit Him in Heaven. He was telling us that we must become aware of His presence. He is always with us, but unless the Spirit helps us, we are often unaware of His presence.

Jesus is the Source of all blessing. He is the fount of all good things. We must deal with Him personally if we are to minister the anointing. We could not ask for any more plain direction. At the time of ministry, get involved with the Lord Jesus, person-to-person and face-to-face, in the Spirit. The Lord is teaching us that the ministry of the anointing requires a focusing upon Him. It calls for a personal experience with Him at the time of the ministering.

Let us note that the Lord does *not* tell us to focus on the Holy Spirit so that the anointing will flow. He clearly says that when we desire the anointing, which is the Holy Spirit, to flow, we must look to Jesus. Come into His presence! Center upon Him!

Later, as we continue to look into the instructions of Jesus in John

7:37-39, we will see that the great emphasis is always to be on the person of the Lord Jesus.

The Holy Spirit has been given to us in order that the Lord Jesus be glorified in us and through us. The Spirit does not seek to glorify Himself, nor does He covet the attention given to the One who sent Him to us. Although we are scripturally authorized to fellowship with the person of the Holy Spirit (see 2 Corinthians 13:14), and we need to do so, when the flow of the anointing is sought, we are to pursue personal relationship with the Lord Jesus. *"Let him come to Me."*

HOW ARE WE TO DO THIS?

The Lord Jesus tells us to become aware of His presence, and to maintain this awareness. During our meetings, in times of anointed worship and adoration, the presence of the Lord is manifested. This is one way in which we come to Him. We do so also by means of anointed prayer in the congregation. But outside of formal meetings (and these are the times in which the members of the Body of Christ sorely need to minister the anointing), we must learn how to come to Him.

Under any and all circumstances, and at any given time or place, believers must know how to come to the awareness of the presence of the Lord Jesus. The anointing is always with us, and always ready to flow — if we do our part to start the flow. And anyone can come into God's presence. There are several ways we do this:

- By praying in tongues and directing our minds and hearts to the Lord Jesus
- By listening to anointed music
- By singing and/or listening to others sing
- By expressing faith in certain scriptural promises. For instance:

I will not leave you as orphans; I will come to you.   John 14:18

Come to me all you who are weary and burdened.   Matthew 11:28

Remain in me, and I will remain in you.   John 15:4

- By turning our attention and our hearts to the Lord Jesus, while relying on the aid of the Holy Spirit

Elijah was one of those in Old Testament times who learned this essential lesson. He is seen, in scripture, coming to King Ahab and making to him an amazing statement. No rain, he said, would come upon the land — *"except at my word"* (1 Kings 17:1). By God's power, the forces of nature regarding rain were to be suspended. In effect, Elijah was ministering the anointing in order that the power of the Spirit could do this mighty deed. Elijah had become an expert on the ministry of the Holy Spirit in power to do whatever was needed at the moment.

Elijah's own words show us that he had learned that the presence of God was required in order to have the anointing flow:

> *And so Elijah the Tishbite, who was of the inhabitants of Gilead, said unto Ahab, As the* LORD *God of Israel lives, BEFORE WHOM I STAND [IN WHOSE PRESENCE I AM], there shall not be dew nor rain these years, but according to my word.*   1 Kings 17:1, KJV

"In whose presence I am." Elijah was in a hostile environment, the royal palace of an enemy king. He was surrounded by the council of nobles who were given to all sorts of pagan practices. He knew that he had to face that situation filled with the presence of God. And it was from that awareness of the presence of God that he was able to minister the Spirit with awesome power.

This principle is even more plainly evidenced in an account of the ministry of the Spirit by Elisha, who had been taught how to do it by Elijah. There was a time when Elisha was called to minister the Spirit in prophecy. Three kings, the evil king of Israel, the godly king of Judah (Jehoshaphat) and the pagan king of Edom, were about to go to war against Moab, a common enemy. They decided to seek a prophecy regarding who would be victorious in the coming battle. Jehoshaphat insisted that they consult with Jehovah for the word they were seeking. Therefore, they sent for Elisha to minister to them.

"Let Him Come to Me"

When the prophet came to meet the three kings, he was angry. He was insulted that two ungodly kings would seek help from the Holy God of Israel. He told them that they ought to go seek help from their false prophets and their false idols they served. In the end, Elisha said that he would minister in prophecy out of respect for King Jehoshaphat. The words he spoke that day echo the principle of the presence of God that his teacher, Elijah, had held forth:

> *Elisha said, "As surely as the LORD Almighty lives, whom I serve [IN WHOSE PRESENCE I AM], if I did not have respect for the presence of Jehoshaphat king of Judah, I would not look at you or even notice you. But now bring me a harpist." While the harpist was playing, the hand of the LORD came upon Elisha.* 2 Kings 3:14-15

Elisha had learned from Elijah to walk in the presence of God so that he would be ready to minister the anointing at all times. At this time, however, he was profoundly disturbed. He was angry. He was overflowing with conflicting emotions.

When he had decided that he would lend his ministry service, the first thing that he realized was that he lacked an awareness of God's presence. Such a lack could prove fatal to the ministry he now wanted to give. He, therefore, had to enter into the awareness of God's presence. This is why he called for a harpist so that holy music could be played. Under the influence of such music, his harsh emotions could settle themselves down, and the presence of God would come upon him once again.

The musician played; Elisha calmed down; and sure enough, the anointing came upon him. Then, he was able to prophesy, and a marvelous miracle resulted (see 2 Kings 3:4-27).

This account is very encouraging. I, too, want to walk in the presence of the Lord constantly, but I find that I do not. There is in me and around me much that works against this desire. I have seen that famous ministers of the anointing also experience similar problems. They do not allow this, however, to prevent them from ministering when the situation calls for it. They simply do what they know is required at the moment, and I have learned to do the same. I seek the presence of the Lord when I seem not to be walking in it at the moment, for in God's presence the anointing will flow.

"Come to Me," says the Lord Jesus, "for Holy Spirit relief from burdens and oppressions." "Come to Me," He says, "when you seek the flow of the anointing to produce needed results."

One of the great promises in the Word of God regarding the activity of the Holy Spirit is found in Isaiah:

> *And it shall come to pass in that day, that his burden shall be taken away from off thy shoulder, and his yoke from off thy neck, and the yoke shall be destroyed because of the anointing.*　　　　　Isaiah 10:27, KJV

Isaiah foretold the time when Messiah, the Anointed One, would come. In that time, he declared, the anointing would lift burdens from men and destroy yokes, or oppressions, in their lives. This was further spelled out in the words of Jesus Himself (the Anointed One).

> *If any man thirst, let him come unto me and drink. He that believeth on me, as the Scripture hath said, out of his belly shall flow rivers of living water [the Holy Spirit].*　　　　　John 7:37-38

> *Come to Me, all you who labor and are heavy laden, and I will give you rest. Take My yoke upon you and learn from Me, for I am gentle and lowly in heart: and you will find rest for your souls. For My yoke is easy and My burden is light.*　　　　　Matthew 11:28-30, NKJ

In the first portion, He said, "*Come unto Me,*" (that the anointing might flow). In the second, He said, "*Come to Me,*" and then went on to tell what the anointing would do. The prophecy of Isaiah 10:27 will be accomplished for us. Unwanted burdens and oppressions will be taken away. This is the work of the anointing. We must come to Jesus so that burdens may be lifted.

Unbelievers and believers alike are subject to burdens and oppressions in this life. Sin and its many consequences, forces of nature that are out of harmony in this present age and demonic activity all cause heavy burdens at times. Sometimes, yokes of heavy oppression hold men in cruel captivity for long periods of time. The Lord has sent the Holy Spirit to us for relief from all these things. His will is that men have rest from such oppressions. And that rest can come only through the power and activity of the Holy Spirit. To obtain such blessings, we are to come to Him. Then, the anointing will flow in power.

In Matthew 11:28, Jesus spoke of deliverance from heavy burdens and from oppressive yokes. Then, in the next two verses, He spoke of a yoke and a burden that He had. He then called us to take upon ourselves His yoke and His burden. His remedy for heavy burdens is to exchange them for His light one.

When Jesus suggested that we take upon ourselves His yoke, He was not saying, as many have believed, that we were to be yoked together with Him, and that together we could pull the loads of life. He was saying that He, too, had experienced a yoke, one that had directed Him in His lifetime. This yoke was not forced upon Him, but He voluntarily assumed it. It then directed Him into the proper burdens for His life. And He was telling His followers that they, too, must be willing to submit to the same yoke that He had taken meekly and humbly. This yoke was, of course, the Spirit of God, through whom Jesus was always in submission to His heavenly Father. He said:

For I have come down from heaven, not to do My own will, but the will of Him who sent Me.   John 6:38, NKJ

Jesus was saying, "The Spirit of God leads Me, guides Me and directs Me in all that the Father wills Me to do. The Spirit is My yoke. Now, you live your life as I have lived Mine. Embrace the way I lived, in submission and obedience to the leading of the Holy Spirit. Take this same yoke I have taken, in meekness and humility of heart. Come to Me."

If we come to Jesus, He says that we can have the power of the anointing to minister against burdensome yokes and oppressions. If we are willing to live our lives in submission to the leadings of the Spirit of God, these burdens will not prevail against us. Our souls will know rest. We will have freedom from the stresses that evil brings to men.

Jesus went on to give us a wonderful guarantee. The yoke of the Spirit will be easy, and the burdens we encounter as we live in the Spirit will be light, even as they were for our Lord.

Jesus showed us that it was a source of strength for Him to live under the yoke of the Holy Spirit:

My food is to do the will of Him who sent Me.   John 4:34, NKJ

Anyone who has taken the Lord at His word understands, by experience, what He promised — peace, joy, delight, contentment and fulfillment. All these abound in one who does as our Lord teaches in these verses.

THE CONTRAST, A CHOICE

The Lord thus shows us the contrast between the yokes and burdens that come in a life lived independently of the Spirit and those burdens that will come as one lives as Jesus lived, led by and obedient to the Spirit. It is as the Old Testament declared:

This day I call heaven and earth as witnesses against you that I have set before you life and death, blessings and curses. Now choose life, so that you and your children may live and that you may love the LORD your God, listen to his voice, and hold fast to him. For the LORD is your life.
                                                                Deuteronomy 30:19-20

Here, the Lord is referring to the realities of human existence in a world that sin has corrupted. Man was created initially to live as a willing subject to a yoke of spiritual origin. The Spirit of God was to be always with him, leading and guiding him in his dominion over creation. He was to live under the yoke of the Holy Spirit, as he lived out the will of the infinitely good Creator for him.

Then, at the fall of Adam, sin and its terrible consequences came upon creation. Burdens and oppressions became a part of human existence. Once the Spirit of God was taken away from men, satanic forces and demon spirits usurped the role of the Spirit. Their influence

46

over the creation, over the race and over individual men has brought to mankind harsh and oppressive yokes, and burdens of all sorts, such as the Creator never intended for men.

So, the message from God to man (His Good News) is just as the Lord implies here. "Take your choice!" We have been created to live, being led by the Holy Spirit in all things, but we now have oppressive burdens and yokes of all sorts because demonic spirits are having their way with us. We must choose one of the two. I, for one, choose the way that will result in blessings and in Holy Spirit power available to me. It is the anointing for the more-than-overcoming life the Lord wants for every one of us.

His yoke will be an easy one for us. His burdens will be light. How beautiful! How far-reaching, the promise of the anointing! "Come to Me," the Lord is saying, "for forgiveness of sin and salvation." "Come to Me," He urges, "for the anointing to flow to lift burdens and destroy yokes."

When the Lord instructs us to come into His presence, this is no mere intellectual knowing that He is with us. We need an awareness of Him, spirit to Spirit, and this can only happen with the aid of the Spirit of God. My human spirit must come to Him and touch Him. And this is to be a matter of reality, not a figment of my imagination. If I expect to see real results, the anointing flowing in power, I must come to Him.

As we have seen, the first step the Lord gave us was that of thirsting for the blessing, a deep and sincere compassion in us. Now, He says, to come to Him. There is to be a heart and spirit touching of Him — a very real spiritual communion taking place. The ministry of the anointing is a matter of much inner activity on the part of the one giving this service.

I readily admit that I am not always as fully and completely involved on these points as I am declaring should be the case. This is the ideal. I admit my human weaknesses and frailties, especially when ministry is to many people, and when the duration of ministry is extended in time. But I praise the Lord for His wonderful grace towards the one needing the ministry. The anointing continues to go forth as I continue to minister, even though my concentration on the required thirsting and on the required coming to the Lord sometimes ebbs and flows. The Lord is calling us to a higher standard, and I, for one, purpose to aim high in order to be an effective agent on His behalf. I want more and more intimacy with the Lord on these matters while serving others.

I would like to point out that this is one of the most delightful aspects regarding ministering the anointing — the deepening intimacy with the Lord that takes place. This intimacy with Him is further dealt with in the next chapter. We will see that there is a "knowing" of God in ministering the anointing that can be described, though inadequately, only by comparing it to the biblical concept of a husband "knowing" his wife in an intimate sexual relationship. In the Spirit, there is a co-mingling of one's being with the Lord Himself.

When I began this ministry eight years ago, I did not have this understanding. As I began to learn to minister the Spirit, I directed my attention, heart and spirit, toward the Lord Jesus. Then I went on to the next three matters, and the anointing began to flow. Anyone can begin as I did, but as I have gone on in this ministering, I see that the intimacy with our Lord is meant to become deeper, and the spiritual delights He gives in this maturing intimacy grow. These are delights that are "better felt then 'telt,' " as the saying goes.

Let me go a bit further on the subject of one of the benefits to a person who is continually ministering the anointing. As I write these words, although I enjoy excellent health, I am seventy-two years old. Due to ministering the anointing, I am experiencing inner delights and seeing spiritual wonders that I could not have imagined twenty or even forty years ago, when my body was much more robust. My point is that the ministry of the anointing has given me something that an older person needs. My productivity and fruitfulness in life were not ended at the age of sixty or even seventy, nor will they end as long as I have breath.

The ministry of the anointing is to last a lifetime. There is no retiring in the Spirit, no being pensioned off. On the contrary, the ministry of the anointing is a matter of increasing intimacy with the Lord Jesus as time passes. It results in greater and greater inner activity as one goes on with it, and the flow of the anointing increases in power and results as one continues to minister. We do, naturally, get older, but the anointing is never old. It is ever young, and it imparts to us a divine youth.

I am determined never to reach that tragic point to which most older

48

people come, when they accept the fact that their best days are behind them. As a result, many of them are filled with resentment, frustration and even depression.

I look at it this way: I am seventy-two years old, and therefore I am much older than many other people are. But I am not OLD! I am young and vigorous on the inside as my intimacy with the Lord grows daily. And the anointing through me is young and robust. It is dynamic and ever more fruitful. This rubs off on me, so that no matter how much older I get, I am never old.

Whatever your age, whatever your present circumstances, begin to act on the Lord's teaching regarding ministering the anointing. If you do, I believe that you will find, as I have, revolutionary meaning and purpose for life. You will discover unique fulfillment where you are right now. And this will continue all the days of your life:

> In returning [to Me] and resting [in Me] you shall be saved;
> in quietness and in [trusting] confidence shall be your strength.
>
> Isaiah 30:15, AMP

This is yet another of the many biblical passages that teach us "*Come to Me.*" As one continues to minister the anointing wherever needs present themselves, he is continually seeking the presence of the Lord Jesus. Such repeated activity leads one into ever-deepening intimacy with Him.

The Lord has led me to take this verse in Isaiah 30 to get further involved with Him personally as I minister the anointing. Since, in order to minister the Spirit, He says "*Come to Me,*" thus I can effectively receive the promise: "*In returning [to Me] and resting [in Me] you shall be saved.*"

"*In returning [to Me]*": When I make the decision to minister the anointing at a given time and place, most often I have been focused on something else entirely. I have been involved with other matters, or with other persons, than the person of the Lord Jesus — and with Him intimately. I then turn away from these concentrations, turn away from these thoughts and interests, and I turn my mental focus back to nothing else but the Lord. As I do this, I am returning to Him in intimacy, and I put away from my awareness all else.

As I focus upon Jesus, I come into intimacy with Him. I have been there often, for I endeavor to do this with Him every morning. Intimacy with the Lord Jesus Christ is the most precious and delightful part of my life. At the moment of ministering, however, intimacy is not just a matter of my personal delight. I need intimacy with the Lord in that moment for the sake of others. I am thirsting for the blessing some other person needs by the anointing, and for this I come to Him in intimacy. I *"return"* to intimacy with Him.

"And resting [in Me]": In this intimacy, I am to come to rest in the Lord regarding the anointing He says will flow from me with power to do the work for which I am thirsting. He is telling me to do certain things (to thirst, to come to Him, to drink, to believe). These are going on within me. Obviously, these activities have no power in themselves to bring on the anointing of the Spirit, much less cause His miracle-working power to act. But I am engaged in them because Jesus says to do so. He has declared, "Do these, My son, and I will see to it that the anointing flows from you in power." Now, as I do them, I am called to rest in Him personally and in the promise of John 7:37-38, that the anointing will flow. I am to rest in the faithfulness of my God, the Lord Jesus, and in His faithfulness to His Word.

Resting in the Lord means that my heart and spirit nuzzle down into the warm faithfulness of the Lord Jesus and His powerful promise.

"You shall be saved": This means you shall be saved from the evil for which you are seeking the power of the anointing. (The Hebrew word translated here as *saved* is *yasha* (pronounced yaw-shah'). It means "to be safe, to be free" and refers to deliverance, to rescue, to be safe, to get victory. This is a word of full and great salvation from evil, not at all merely forgiveness of sins. It is akin to the Greek word *sozo* that is used in the New Testament to encompass the great salvation brought by Messiah, the Christ, the Anointed One. It speaks of salvation from every kind of evil and from their consequences. (*Strong's Concordance,* and also *Wilson's Old Testament Word Studies.*)

The Messiah, the Christ, with the anointing of the Spirit, came to save me in this very broad scope of the concept of salvation. This is the very same Holy Spirit anointing that the Lord has given to me. This anointing will do through me things that the Holy Spirit did through

Jesus, as I do the things He has commanded me to do. When I am ministering the anointing, therefore, I am resting in His words.

"In quietness and in [trusting] confidence shall be your strength."

"In quietness": I do not propose to take issue here with the way other men minister the anointing. When the Holy Spirit flows in power to do miracles, He is doing them because He wants to. No man is forcing the Spirit to act against His will. What human could do such a thing? May the anointing and the power of the Spirit and the glory of God cover the earth, even as the waters cover the seas — however it comes!

Some minister the anointing with much music and singing. Some run excitedly to and fro on the platform or even up and down the aisles of the building. Some scream loudly as they call for the anointing to fall. Some shout out over and over, even dozens of times: "In the name of Jesus." Some do much stranger things as the Spirit leads them, and when they do, the anointing goes forth. Let men do as the Lord leads them, and let God be God.

But, in this book, I am focusing on John 7:37-39. Here the Lord teaches us to do four things to minister the anointing. They are things that can be done in quiet, without fanfare, for they happen within the person ministering. The anointing will flow as these four things are done, without any of the many external activities that have often been associated with it. The anointing will flow in great power in places and situations that have no religious connection. It will flow with no previous preparation, no planning, and with no musicians or choral groups present. Jesus did not speak of any physical or material preparations that were required.

No showy intensity of attitude and no loud voice is needed. The intensity that the Lord requires in these two verses is to be within the person ministering: thirsting, coming to Him, drinking and believing on Him. By concentrating on these four things alone, one can achieve the flow of the anointing. This is Jesus' teaching, that ANYONE who does as He says will see the works of the Spirit through his or her life.

Personally, when ministering the anointing, I am usually very quiet externally. At the same time, I am active internally within my spirit, as I relate to the Lord *"in [trusting] confidence."*

In ministering the anointing, one needs to have confidence in the Lord that the anointing will indeed flow. As one begins to minister, he or she may not feel any spiritual motions within, nor even feel very spiritual at all. We will deal with this at length in the chapter on the fourth point the Lord presents in order to minister the anointing: *"Believe in Me."*

In this part of Isaiah 30:15, I have found a way to build my confidence and expectancy that the anointing is about to flow. Leaning on the Spirit and in the intimacy with the Lord into which I have now entered, I begin to express my trust in Him and His Word and my confidence that He will indeed cause the Spirit to flow. This, I have found, needs to be done before the anointing flows.

As I continue relating with the Lord in this way, I begin to sense in my spirit a confidence which was not present at the outset of ministry. I sense a deep trust in Him and in His Word, and, as He promised, this *"confidence shall be your strength."*

Dealing in this way with these four matters in Isaiah 30 has now brought me to a place of inner strength and expectancy that the anointing is about to flow. More than that, I have now reached a position of great strength regarding the anointing. I have concentrated on what the Lord has told me to do. I have not added external things that might serve to "work up" my feelings, nor the feelings of others. I have truly been working in the awareness of my own weakness to cause the anointing. I have been leaning on the Spirit and the Lord Jesus only. Thus, the promise of the Word comes to pass: *"My grace is sufficient for you, for my power is made perfect in weakness"* (2 Corinthians 12:9).

Let us remember that the Lord teaches that in ministering the anointing, our focus must be on Him. Let us then come to Him, who says to us, *"I am the life"* (John 14:6). Whatever we are seeking in the power of the Spirit, the divine life of the Lord Jesus is its source. Let us come to Him. As He told the Samaritan woman in John 4, the spring of living water that He placed in us when He gave each the Holy Spirit will now begin to well up. The eternal life of God will begin to flow out.

> *He who comes to me will never go hungry, and he who believes in me will never be thirsty.* John 6:35

Hear the Lord's voice today, *"Come to Me!"*

CHAPTER 4

"AND DRINK"

"If anyone is thirsty, let him come to me AND DRINK. Whoever believes in me, as the Scripture has said, streams of living water will flow from within him." By this he meant the Spirit. John 7:37-39

In this passage that teaches us how to minister the anointing, we have seen that the Lord gives us very simple instructions. He has said that this ministry is for ANYONE, that the person is to THIRST after the blessing sought from the power of the Holy Spirit, and that he is to COME to the Lord Jesus personally. Now, we see the next step — "DRINK."

What could be more simple? DRINK. But ... drink what?

Jesus has used the image of living waters to refer to the anointing which is to come forth from the believer who is ministering. The effect of what the believer is doing is to be the flowing forth of the anointing, just as water flows. I do not believe, however, that He is now telling the believer to drink of the flowing water that is the Holy Spirit. Let me explain why:

1. The anointing is not yet flowing. What we are doing is attempting to get the flow going. The drinking is one of the steps He tells us to take in order that this flowing begin. He is not saying to drink of the Holy Spirit in order to have the Holy Spirit become active. In one sense, the Holy Spirit has not yet come on the scene for activity. Although He is always there, we have not yet tapped into His flow.

2. Jesus has just told the person ministering to come to Him personally. The minister is to be intimately involved with the Lord Jesus. He is, therefore, the One who is to be the object of this drinking. He has said, *"Come to Me,"* and now He is saying what is to be done upon coming to Him.

Jesus is not saying that we should drink of the Holy Spirit (although the Spirit will indeed flow forth just as waters flow). He is telling us to come to Him, and in His presence, to drink of Him. He is life Himself, the life that we need. He is the Source of all provision. We need to partake of His life in order that the Spirit, whom He has given us, might flow forth from us with power. So, He says, "Do this: Drink of Me, and I will see to it that the anointing flows forth from you, even as waters flow."

I want to explain further what it means to drink of the Lord Jesus, and will show portions of His Word that deal with this, one of the truly inscrutable mysteries in the Word of God. But before dealing with these concepts, let me point out that to minister the anointing, all the Lord requires is that we drink of Him. He does not say that we must have a great understanding of all that the Scriptures reveal about this profound subject.

HOW TO DRINK THE LORD JESUS

To cause the anointing to flow from us, the Lord tells us to drink of Him. Notice that He is instructing us to do something, to perform some act. His example is of a person who has a glass of water in his hand and puts it to his lips. The person then begins to draw the water into himself by using a sucking motion.

Soon, the water begins to flow, and then swallowing commences and continues as long as the supply lasts and the sucking continues. The water then, having come into the person, goes about its work effecting the consequences in the body that water always produces.

Let me point out an obvious reality concerning this example. The water in the glass, or the water that has come to the lips of a person, is of no avail to his body unless and until he begins to suck it into his body. It is not the closeness of the water to him that gives its blessing to his body. The closeness is important, but it is not enough. Unless there is an act of receiving the water into the body, it cannot do any good.

We can carry over this example to the ministry of the anointing. The Lord has told us to come to Him, to come into His presence. This is like being in the same room as a glass of water. It is now available. But unless we receive it and take it into ourselves, it does us no good. In the same way, we must receive from the Lord — drink Him in.

Of course, we cannot drink the physical body of the Lord. That can't be done. But when we are in His presence in the Spirit, we can draw Him into ourselves by our faith and desire.

The delights of the Spirit-manifested presence of the Lord Jesus are widely known and sought after, but to cause the anointing to flow out from us, there must be an active drawing of Him into us, spirit to Spirit. This is the drinking of Him. It is a drinking of faith which can be performed by our thirsty souls. When we do it, in some marvelous way, the Spirit of Jesus becomes more and more co-mingled with our human spirits.

This is far less complicated to do than it may sound. Once we have come into the Lord's presence and have opened ourselves wholly to Him, we can begin to drink, to draw Him into us. Then we draw, and draw and draw some more, and we are more and more filled with Him. You can even sense it happening, and again, it is "better felt than 'telt.' "

With your mind, with your heart and with your spirit, draw the Lord into yourself. Don't waste time trying to analyze this wonder of wonders. Simply do it. Try it. You will be surprised how easy it is and how wonderful it is.

When you drink a glass of water, you don't worry about exactly where it goes and what it does or how it does it. You just enjoy it and let it do its work. You feel refreshed. You feel renewed. And you trust that the water will accomplish its purpose. So it is with drinking the Lord Jesus. Drink Him in, and then trust Him to cause the anointing to flow out from you in power.

When you want to minister the anointing, therefore, come to the

Lord and begin to drink of Him, and very quickly you will be ready to go on to the next of the Lord's directions — to believe on Him.

Now, let's delve further into this matter of drinking the Lord Jesus.

OTHER SCRIPTURAL CONFIRMATION

One of the basic concepts of the Word of God (and one that is vital for every believer) is that we should have life, and life more abundantly in the Kingdom of God. The life we seek is in Jesus, for He is life. Life continually flows in Him, and if we allow it to, it will flow from Him to us. It is this life that will bring forth from us multiplied fruit to bless us and others. This is the elemental teaching of many biblical passages, such as John 6:25-66, 10:10, 14:6 and 15:1-10 and 2 Corinthians 3:18, Galatians 2:20, Philippians 3:8-11 and many others.

For instance:

Where shall we buy bread for these people to eat?   John 6:5

Human beings need food to supply the energy needed so that their bodies and souls can perform as they were designed. And we need food continually — more than once a day, and every day. Depending on the amount of activity, our bodies can quickly come to the place that they must replenish their energy supply by taking food into themselves or else they will be severely weakened. This is the picture presented in John 6:1-14.

A large crowd had gathered to hear Jesus' teachings, and they had not eaten for several days. They needed food, and there was no place to get it. They were in a remote area where they could not buy anything to eat.

This was a desperate situation, and Jesus showed His compassion for the need of the people by supernaturally providing their needs. They ate and were filled, and their bodies received the nourishment they needed to continue functioning.

That chapter goes on to explain that God has a full supply for man — spirit, soul and body. He can provide our every need. Our needs are not only physical. They are spiritual, emotional and material, and God has made provision for them all. He wants every part of us to be functioning well for Him.

The most basic necessity of man is Jesus. He is our nourishment. It is His life in us that will bring us to full maturity. He is the full provision for all of our needs.

In verses 25-35, the emphasis is upon *"doing the works of God."* Some religious leaders came to Jesus and asked Him what they could do to work the works of God. They were concerned about what religious acts were acceptable to Him. The Lord answered them that the work of God is to believe in the One God sent (verse 29).

For a long time, I wondered at this answer. I was focusing on the believing that a person must do in order to become saved. But surely, I reasoned, there had to be more to doing the works of God than simply getting saved. Didn't a person have more to do in life that would be pleasing to God than just believing on Jesus for salvation?

One day, while the Lord was opening up to me some of the riches contained in John 7: 37, I finally began to understand what He was saying in John 6:29. In John 7:37, I am called to come to the Lord Jesus, to drink Him and to believe on Him. If I do that, the Holy Spirit will come forth to lift burdens, destroy oppressive yokes, and to do positive and constructive works through the Spirit. These are the works of God that He desires to see us doing today.

God has fashioned us so that we may be His agents, those who do His works, and He Himself is willing to dwell within His agents. He has chosen to involve men in His acts. It is not the person doing the work, but the Lord Jesus, by His Spirit, does the work by going forth from the person and causing the happenings. His divine power performs the works through those who believe in Him.

Jesus was teaching those religious leaders that men, acting alone and with their own natural talents and abilities, cannot do works that please God. We need God, by His Spirit, to act through us, and He will — as we submit ourselves to Him.

The works of God, therefore, are works done by God. Works done by man are just that — man's works. They can never be the works of God. This is an important teaching for all believers, and many are yet ignorant of it. They sincerely want to do works that please God, but because they don't know how to let God work through them, they continue to do their own works. This is tragic, for our own works are as worthless to God as those being done by the religious Jews of Jesus' day.

So, in verses 1-14, we see that men need food in order to function properly. In verses 24-34, we see that to do the works of God, God must be in us and must be working through us. Then, in verses 35-63, we see the means by which men can be involved in doing the works of God. It requires that the Lord Jesus, the life of God, be acting through us by the Spirit.

In verse 29, Jesus said that men were to believe in Him so that the works of God would be done through them. Going on, He explained, in parable form, how to do this. In verse 32, He showed that God has given to men the real bread, the real nourishment, that will enable us to have the provision we need in all matters of life. This food will become in us divine power and energy that can then work through us, even as natural bread produces a natural energy in our bodies. Those who eat this food that God has sent will be found doing the works of God.

> *Jesus said to them, "I tell you the truth, it is not Moses who has given you the bread from heaven, but it is my Father who gives you the true bread from heaven."*
> John 6:32

Jesus went on to tell exactly what was this food from Heaven that would provide marvelous life:

> *For the bread of God is he who comes down from heaven and gives life to the world.*
> *I am the bread of life.*
> John 6:33 and 35

Jesus, who also said He was the life of God (see John 14:6), is teaching us how vital this life is to us. It is just as vital as the food we eat every day. Just as we eat regularly to have the physical nourishment our bodies need, we must also partake of Him. In this sense, He is to be eaten, to be ingested.

A miraculous material food was given to the Jewish people in the

"And Drink"

wilderness. It gave them physical energy to perform their needed functions. In this same way, men need the spiritual food, which is the life of God, for strength for all things in their daily living. And, as the Lord has said, He is that food, the food that results in the life of God flowing through men and manifesting itself in them and through them.

Jesus said, *"I am the bread of life."* When we eat natural bread, we are then able to function. Although we act, however, it is the energy from the bread that is enabling us to do it. Without that energy, we could not function. In one sense, they are our acts, but in another sense, they are not. They are expressions of the energy of the bread. The energy we have today is a result of the meals we ate yesterday or the day before. We are living, but it is also the energy of the bread that is living in us. This is what is required to do the works of God — the energy of Him who is our bread working in us. He is that bread. So eat.

In verse 35, we again see the invitation of Jesus to come to Him. It is to eat of the bread which He provides, the bread which He is, so that we can have His energy working through us. John 7:37 tells us to come and drink. The meaning is the same. By faith, we take the Lord Jesus and all that He represents into our lives, and then the life of God is in us and the works of God will be done through us. This will be true of whatever we happen to be doing at the time. The anointing will flow out from us to accomplish the needed task.

There is a wonderful guarantee offered with this teaching:

> *He who comes to me will never go hungry, and he who believes in me will never be thirsty!*   John 6:35

If we come to Him, believe in Him and partake of Him, then we will never go without the provision we seek. The Holy Spirit will flow out from us as water flows — always. The anointing will flow out of us to do the works of God on our own behalf and on the behalf of others — always.

This promise is to ANYONE. WHOEVER comes to Jesus for provision will never be disappointed. The anointing will be continually active in you and through you to lift burdens and to provide supply where there is lack.

Just as you feel the need to eat often, partake of the Lord often. Renew your energy source. Do it regularly. Then you will have energy for the many works God wants to do through you.

Verse 40 is powerful:

> *For my Father's will is that everyone who looks to the Son and believes in him*
> *shall have eternal life.* John 6:40

This is the Father's will, that eternal life, the life of God, be flowing in you, as you eat of the living bread and drink of the living water.

Jesus said it again in verse 54:

> *Whoever eats my flesh and drinks my blood has eternal life.* John 6:54

The person who has the life of God in him has the potential to work the works of God. The anointing is in him to express God's will often and continually.

> *Whoever eats my flesh and drinks my blood remains in me, and I in him.*
> John 6:56

Eating and drinking of the Lord will cause us to *"remain"* in Him. Other translations use the word *"abide."* Coming to the Lord and abiding in Him entails not only being in His presence, but also partaking of Him in the Spirit. This truth is spelled out in John 15:1-10, where Jesus gives us the parable of the true vine and teaches us about our being branches in the vine. In that passage, also, He gives us the command to abide, or remain, in Him.

John 6:56 very clearly shows us what abiding, or remaining, in the Lord means. It is coming into His presence and, spirit to Spirit, partaking of Him, taking Him to ourselves.

The parable of the true vine teaches us the same truth. The branch that has been grafted into the vine has indeed come to the vine intimately, and it is open to the vine and actively taking to itself the sap, the life, of the vine. The branch is abiding in the vine because of doing two things: (1) It has come to the vine, and (2) It is drawing to itself the life of the vine. Note in this example the Lord gave that the branch has not merely come into union with the vine. It is vital for the branch to take to itself what the vine now offers — its sap. Only then will fruit result.

This same thing is true regarding our relationship to the Lord Jesus. We have been grafted into the vine. We have been joined with Jesus. To produce fruit, we must have His life flowing continually into us. Merely being in His presence, as wonderful as that is, is not enough. The active taking of Him to ourselves by faith must be done. Then, we will be abiding in Him and drinking from Him. We have far more than a dry connection to the vine.

This is the only way to live the Christian life — by always abiding in Him for all things. We can do nothing without Him, and He made that abundantly clear. There is no fruit possible without the life that comes from the vine.

This, then, is true also of the ministry of the anointing. To have it, we must abide in Him. We must come to know Him intimately and to partake of Him constantly by faith. Only then will the anointing work through us. *"Come to Me AND DRINK."*

The Lord Jesus is saying here in John 6:56 exactly what He said in John 15:4. If we abide in Him (that is, coming to Him and eating or drinking of Him by faith), He gives us a guarantee. He will cause the flow of His life into our beings and through our beings. Then, out from our innermost parts, where the Holy Spirit dwells in us, the anointing will come with power to do the things for which we are thirsting.

It would be well for each of us to study more fully these two requirements of the Christian life that I have outlined here. And let us live them continually, as we abide in the Lord Jesus. As Jesus taught us in John 15:1-12, let us live, continually drawing upon the life of the Lord.

The challenge goes out to one and all — *"If anyone thirst, let him come to Me and drink."* Now, we will see one more thing the Lord says is vitally important to the flow of the anointing in our lives — *"Believe in Me."*

CHAPTER 5

"HE WHO **BELIEVES** IN ME"

"If anyone is thirsty, let him come to me and drink. WHOEVER BELIEVES IN ME, as the Scripture has said, streams of living water will flow from within him." By this he meant the Spirit. John 7:37-39

ANYONE who thirsts for a blessing that the Holy Spirit has come to earth to provide is welcome to come and drink. There is, however, one added requirement. This promise is for those who will believe in the Lord Jesus. When we believe, the anointing will come forth to work that needed blessing.

Believe in Him ... Before we go any further, let us pause to look at the simplicity of this command. Having obediently carried out several other simple steps — thirsting, coming to Jesus and partaking of Him — now the Lord is teaching that the anointing will flow as we believe His promise that it will do so.

The Lord has spoken His directions. We have heard them and done them. Now, we are to believe that the result He promised will indeed come to pass.

By believing Him, we are accepting His personal integrity. He is the Truth personified. He is totally trustworthy. He is the absolute rock of faithfulness. I must choose to believe His promise. I must believe His person.

BELIEVING IN HIS PROMISE

"The word is near you; it is in your mouth and IN YOUR HEART," that is,

"He Who BELIEVES in Me"

the word of faith we are proclaiming: That if you confess with your mouth, "Jesus is Lord," and believe IN YOUR HEART that God raised him from the dead, you will be saved. For it is WITH YOUR HEART that you believe and are justified, and it is with your mouth that you confess and are saved. As the Scripture says, "Anyone who trusts in him will never be put to shame."
Romans 10:8-11

Believing a word of God, a promise of God, is done with our hearts. It is a belief in the innermost part of our beings. Mere mental acceptance of a matter is not enough. We must see with the understanding what the Word is saying and then believe with our hearts that it is indeed so.

For the fruit of a given word, or promise, of God to come about, the seed of that word must penetrate into the understanding and the heart. It must be seen there, accepted there and depended upon there if fruit is to result.

Here, in Romans, Paul speaks of the word which brings us salvation. We must understand it, believe it in our hearts and then speak it with our mouths. The promise is that fruit will result.

In John 7:37, the word spoken by the Lord Jesus promises wonderful fruit: the anointing of the Holy Spirit going forth from an individual to do a work of divine power. The Lord promises that ANYONE who does the heart activities of thirsting, coming to Him and drinking Him will have this result. It will not come, however, without faith on our part. We must get God's Word well planted in our hearts.

The Scriptures teach that this is done by meditation on a word, or promise (see Psalm 1:2-3, Mark 4:8, 20 and 24-25). A word, when it is planted in our spirits in this way, constantly speaks to us. It enables us to see and hear what we are believing for. This is what the Lord is calling for in John 7:37-38. Believe in your heart that what He is promising will happen, and it will.

This is such a simple matter. You can say, "Lord Jesus, I have done the three things You told me to do in order that the anointing flow. Now, the matter is in Your hands to cause the Holy Spirit to act. I believe Your promise, Lord, and I wait expectantly." I address the Lord in this way often, and He responds, proving that He is faithful to His Word.

BELIEVE IN THE PERSON OF THE LORD JESUS

We must go beyond believing a promise. We must believe the Promisor. Fix your attention on Him personally. From your heart, depend on Him personally to cause the flow of the anointing from you. He has told us to come to Him, to come to the awareness of His presence. He has told us to drink of Him, to draw Him to ourselves by our hearts and spirits. Then, He says to believe in Him, to depend on Him. When we have done this, the Spirit will flow with power to do the thing for which one is thirsting. An intimate, person-to-person depending on the Lord Jesus is involved in the ministry of the anointing.

Hebrews 3:1 shows us that we must consider Jesus: *"fix your thoughts on [Him]."* This is what we do in believing in Him, and it is to be done person-to-person. As I wait for the Spirit to move, and even as He begins to do so, I remain personally involved with the Lord Jesus. If there is a matter of ministry to several or to many people, this is how I occupy myself till the ministry has been completed. In the words of the Scriptures, I *"look"* to the Lord Jesus while I am laying hands on people for the anointing to flow and to continue flowing.

> *... Looking unto Jesus, the author and finisher of our faith ...*
> Hebrews 12:2, NKJ

The ministering of the anointing requires a continual looking unto Him. In this same way, Jesus ministered the anointing. He, of course, looked to His Father.

> *Looking up to heaven, He blessed and broke and gave the loaves to the disciples.*
> Matthew 14:19, NKJ

Our Lord explained this concept of looking unto God during His ministry of the anointing:

> *I tell you the truth, the Son can do nothing by himself; he can do only what he sees his Father doing, because whatever the Father does the Son also does.*
> John 5:19
> (See also Mark 7:34.)

64

"He Who BELIEVES in Me"

This same principle is expressed in the Psalms:

I lift up my eyes to you, to you whose throne is in heaven.
As the eyes of slaves look to the hand of their master,
as the eyes of a maid look to the hand of her mistress,
so our eyes look to the LORD our God,
till he shows us his mercy.   Psalm 123:1-2

The eyes of our hearts should look to the Lord until He grants us the anointing of power we seek.

Never allow yourself to be filled with thoughts of the magnitude of the problem for which you are seeking the power of the Spirit. Do not center your attention on the gravity of the sickness for which you seek healing, for instance. Do not focus your attention on doubts, worries or anxieties. Do not think of the possibility that the anointing may not flow in the matter before you.

You have done what the Lord told you to do in order for the anointing to be manifested. Now, fix your mind and heart on Him. Dependence on Him is all that is needed as you await the flow of the anointing. Expressions of love, adoration and worship toward Him (as you are depending on Him) will serve to keep negative thoughts away from you.

So that the anointing may flow from you, the Lord does not call for much shouting, nor for repeated religious sayings. Some use the phrase "in the name of Jesus" over and over. While it is not wrong to do this, there is nothing we can do to force the anointing to come forth.

The Lord does not tell us to work up our emotions or the emotions of those to whom we are ministering. His instructions in John 7:37-39 make no mention of such activity, and His own examples in the Scriptures, when He ministered the Spirit, do not show such fleshly behavior.

Most assuredly, we must understand our own weakness and inability to cause the Holy Spirit to become active through us. No matter what we do of our own efforts — straining and shouting — we cannot force the Spirit's activity. In the awareness of our weakness, our personal helplessness to cause the flow of living waters, however, we can do what the Lord says: believe in Him, depend on Him, fill your thoughts with Him! This will put you in the ideal position for the flow of the Spirit.

We can even rejoice in our obvious weakness! This very awareness of our weakness now becomes our strength. The Lord has said:

My grace is sufficient for you, for my power is made perfect in weakness.

2 Corinthians 12:9

We are commanded:

Ask the LORD for rain in the spring time;
it is the LORD who makes the storm clouds.
He gives showers of rain to men,
and plants of the field to everyone.   Zechariah 10:1

God gives natural rain to the needy earth. It does not come by the efforts and strainings of the flesh, nor by expressions of the natural strengths of men. If God doesn't send it, there is none. It is the same with the needed rain of the Spirit. Do what the Lord says to do without adding fleshly efforts. Then the Spirit will flow in power.

ACT IN ACCORD WITH YOUR BELIEVING

When we believe, we must act according to our faith. We must speak according to our faith. In this respect, Elijah gives us a clear lesson regarding ministering the anointing. We noted earlier that he ministered from the presence of God. Now, let us focus on his behavior and his words at the time:

And Elijah the Tishbite, who was of the inhabitants of Gilead, said unto Ahab, As the LORD God of Israel live, before whom I stand [in whose presence I am], there shall not be dew nor rain these years, but according to my word.

1 Kings 17:1, KJV

Elijah had heard from God regarding what the Holy Spirit would do

66

to the weather in Israel. He believed God and acted accordingly. He went to King Ahab, relying on what he had heard and relying upon the faithfulness of God. When he arrived before the king, He boldly spoke forth his belief. He was engaged in the ministry of the Spirit in power. In this case, it was power to cause rain to cease in the land. The prophet thus put himself at great risk by coming to Ahab with his bold words, for they were in opposition to the idolatrous leader.

Note that Elijah was speaking out words that declared what the Holy Spirit was going to do. There was, as yet, no material evidence of what he was declaring. He was not only putting himself at risk as he opposed the king, but he was putting his reputation as a prophet at risk as well. If the Holy Spirit did not act as he was saying, his ministry would "go down the tubes"!

Elijah was acting on his faith. He was speaking by his faith, and he was doing it boldly. This is the proper way to minister the anointing. Believe in the words of the Lord, and in Him. Then speak forth the bold declaration of your faith; divine power will flow.

As an example, you might declare, "In the name of Jesus, the Holy Spirit now comes upon you to [do such a matter]." "At my word, the Holy Spirit heals you." "Now, the anointing comes upon you [for the particular supply sought]."

The Lord so ministered the Spirit with bold words:

"Lazarus, come forth!"   John 11:43, NKJ

Note in verse 41 that He looked unto His Father as He ministered the anointing. Peter learned this lesson from his Master:

Silver and gold have I none; but such as I have give I thee: In the name of Jesus Christ of Nazareth rise up and walk.   Acts 3:6, KJV

Peter did not have healing to give, but He did have the Spirit of healing to give. He ministered the anointing with bold words, and the lame man was healed. He declared openly that He was imparting the anointing then and there, and it worked.

One who would minister the anointing is to speak forth his or her faith boldly. There is to be a bold declaration regarding what the Holy Spirit is now flowing out to do, and these words are to be spoken, even *before* one senses the anointing flowing out.

When I am ministering the anointing, I sometimes sense the anointing before I declare what the Holy Spirit will then do. But sometimes I declare the anointing is now flowing before I am sensing the flow. In both cases, I have done what the Lord has required — thirsting, coming to Him and drinking of Him. Then I speak my faith, regardless of what I am sensing. I have found that the Lord always responds as He said He would, and the anointing flows. It has happened to me countless times now. I have also seen many thousands of others achieve the same results, as they follow these simple steps that the Lord Jesus sets forth for us.

CHAPTER 6

"AS THE SCRIPTURE HAS SAID"

"If anyone is thirsty, let him come to me and drink. Whoever believes in me,
AS THE SCRIPTURE HAS SAID, streams of living water will flow from
within him." By this he meant the Spirit. John 7:37-39

The Lord is saying that the ministry of the anointing of the Holy Spirit was spoken of in the Old Testament scriptures. To what particular scripture did He refer? Where in the Word of God do we find flowing living water as the symbol of the Holy Spirit working? And where is it found that the Holy Spirit is flowing out of men to do such works? This beautiful picture is presented in chapter 47 of the book of Ezekiel.

In chapters forty through forty-six of this book, the prophet sets forth the directions He received regarding the rebuilding of the Temple in Jerusalem. The Jews had been in captivity in Babylon since the Temple was destroyed by the invaders.

Then, in chapter 47, Ezekiel recounted a vision that he had of another temple, one to come far in the future. In this vision, he saw a temple from which waters were flowing forth.

These were unique waters. For in and of themselves they caused life to appear and to flourish wherever they flowed. These waters were, in no way, natural waters. They began as a mere trickle coming forth from the Temple, but marvelously, as they flowed, they actually increased in depth and in width. Ultimately, as they continued on, they divided and formed various rivers.

These waters had life in them, and they brought life to wherever, whatever and whomever they touched. They flowed into the Dead Sea (where no life can exist because of the excessively high salinity), and the sea was changed into fresh water. Suddenly, it was capable of sustaining life, and its waters were teeming with life:

> ... *where the river flows everything will live.*   Ezekiel 47:9

These living waters then flowed forth and caused growth, abundance, fruitfulness, prosperity and blessings of all sorts wherever they touched.

There is a somber implication in verse 11 for all those who call themselves Christians. For where these waters are present but not flowing (as in marshes and swamps), life disappears! In stagnation, there again appears death. The flow of the anointing, which is the activity of the Holy Spirit, causes life to be manifested. This is the flow of the life of God. The anointing flow results in life all around it, and a lack of flow results in a lack of life. All of us need the ministry of the anointing, and we need it to flow to ourselves and through us to others.

In the vision, the flow of these living waters produces trees. This is highly significant. Trees are the greatest organisms in the plant kingdom. The living waters bring forth not mere plants, grasses, nor bushes, but trees.

Trees are tall, strong and majestic. They have deep, well-developed root structures, which hold them firm in whatever storms or hardships they may face.

The trees Ezekiel saw were fruit-bearing. They had leaves for their own beauty, and they also bore abundant fruit for the needs of many others. The flow of the anointing is for abundance of blessings to all it touches. Those who receive it for themselves will grow in all ways and develop strong foundations. They will prosper, and they will have abundance of supply to give to others. They will be anointed with the Holy Spirit. Their cups will be full, and they will be overflowing for others.

The Lord Jesus refers to this vision of Ezekiel when He says that rivers of living water will flow out from within those who do as He says. Ezekiel saw the living waters flowing out from a temple. These two came together on the Day of Pentecost. The disciples were present at the Temple in Jerusalem, as were all pious Jews on that morning. The Holy Spirit came upon the Lord's followers in a mighty anointing, filling them, and thereafter remaining within them. Collectively, they became *"the temple of the Holy Spirit."* Also, individually, each became a temple of the Holy Spirit.

The temple ceased to be a structure made of stone and became flesh. God dwells in men and works through men. He expects His Spirit to flow from each of us during our lifetimes.

From that new temple (formed by the believers), the Holy Spirit began to flow that day in great power to accomplish His works in the earth, even as did the living waters in the prophetic vision that was given to Ezekiel centuries before. As believers went forth, and wherever they went, the anointing continued to flow from them. Life resulted wherever the flow went.

This flow has gone on now for some two thousand years. It has become deep and wide in the earth. Now, in the present day, so close to the return of the Lord, the flow of the anointing is poised for the culmination of its flowing forth from converted sinners. This last and greatest activity of the anointing will be accomplished through millions of believers.

Let every temple of the Spirit take his or her place as one who has been indwelt by the Spirit, so that the anointing may flow forth continually from each one of them. The glory of God will cover the earth as never before in this age. This is why the Spirit has come to you!

CHAPTER 7

IN SUMMARY

*"If anyone is thirsty, let him come to me and drink. Whoever believes in me,
as the Scripture has said, streams of living water will flow from within him."
By this he meant the Spirit.* John 7:37-39

The Lord Jesus has given directions regarding the ministry of the anointing. He has directed us to do certain things. If we do those things, He guarantees that the anointing will then flow in power.

THINGS HE DOES NOT REQUIRE

Some of the things we commonly think of as prerequisites for the anointing are notably absent from the Lord's instructions. I have specifically examined many of them and found that they are not required for the anointing to flow. They are not prerequisites for the ministry of the anointing.

I have noticed, for instance, that the Lord does not say that the Holy Spirit will flow:

- If you are fasting
- If you have prayed much
- If you have interceded greatly
- If you have not sinned in a given period of time
- If you are a longtime believer
- If you have read your Bible regularly, or at length
- If you are a deacon or an elder in the church

In Summary

- If you are an ordained minister
- If you are in a religious atmosphere, for instance, in a church meeting
- If you have done works for the Lord

He does not require any of these things in order for the anointing to flow!

It is not my intention to speak against these or any other matters that form part of the life of believers. Nor is it my purpose in this book to point out where and how each of these may be highly desirable, or even vitally necessary for us as believers. The purpose of this book is to underline and to stress the four things the Lord says anyone is to do in order to cause the anointing to flow. When those four things are sincerely acted upon, the Holy Spirit goes into action.

There is no need to set forth as prerequisites for Holy Spirit ministry practices other than these four, however desirable they may be for Christian living. The Lord tells us to do four things. Do them, and the Holy Spirit will flow in power for anyone.

I have ministered the anointing on a full stomach and also when I was fasting. In both cases, the Holy Spirit flowed. I have ministered after a time of prayer, and I have also ministered after a time of playing a computer game. In both cases, the Holy Spirit flowed. I have ministered the anointing in a church building after teaching the Word of God and having a time of worship, but I have also ministered the Spirit in taxicabs, in barbershops, on jet planes, in kitchens and on street corners. Regardless of the physical setting, the Holy Spirit flowed.

I have ministered after I had a time of intercession, and I have also ministered in situations which I was newly confronting. In both cases, the Holy Spirit flowed. I have taught longtime believers how to minister the anointing, and I have also taught believers who were only minutes old in the Kingdom. In both cases, the Holy Spirit flowed. I have taught believers who had been hungry for years to minister the anointing, and on at least one occasion, I taught a man who, ten minutes before, had strongly confessed his atheism. In each case, the anointing flowed. I have taught students of the Bible to minister the Spirit, and I have also taught people who have been ignorant of the Bible. In both cases, the Holy Spirit flowed.

Again, I am not teaching on the things needed in the Christian life, and I will not even bother to mention things that I do personally, which I consider to be vital to my Christian walk. I am simply analyzing the Lord's instructions on how anyone and everyone can minister the anointing.

The simple truth is that after years of teaching thousands of people how to minister the anointing, I have found that the instructions of the Lord in John 7:37-38 lack nothing. His four steps are complete. Anyone who thirsts may come to Him and believe on Him and see results.

We must be careful not to always insist on our own pet practices and make them prerequisites for this ministry. We must try the Lord's way and see what results it will bring us. This does not mean that we stop walking out in our daily lives the steps that are necessary for Christian growth.

SOME SIMPLE CONCLUSIONS

These first chapters have all dealt with the truths of John 7:37-39, which contain the instructions of the Lord as to how anyone can minister the anointing. The power of God will then cause things to happen in them and through them. There are no special words that need to be said as one is ministering the Holy Spirit. There also is no rigid order in dealing with the four things the Lord says to do. Nor must one regularly follow the same order when he ministers.

There is not even always the need to deal with all four steps each time one ministers the anointing. For learning purposes, I believe it is wise and desirable to get involved with all of the four as one is learning this ministry. There is no set prayer that one must copy or follow. There are these four matters of the heart that are to be dealt with. Humility and sincerity of heart regarding each of them is called for. From such heart activity will come forth the words apt for the ministry at hand.

But, for learning purposes, let me present an example of such words for ministry of the anointing, words that one might be led to speak for the ministry of healing:

In Summary

Lord Jesus,

I desire deeply, I thirst that the Holy Spirit anointing now flow for healing (name the person who is receiving and address the specific need).
I come to You, Lord — into Your presence — so that the flow of the anointing might come forth. (Now, come to the awareness of His presence.)
Here and now, Lord, I drink of You. My spirit draws You, Lord Jesus, to me. And I believe Your words, Lord Jesus, in John 7. I believe in You. I depend on You that the anointing will now flow.

I then say to the person to whom I am ministering:

What I have I give to you — the Spirit of healing. The anointing for healing now comes upon you to heal you, right now!

In the name of Jesus.

The person or persons receiving the anointing must be open to receive from the Lord Jesus. This openness to receive from Him is basic. To receive this blessing, a person does not need great faith. Mustard-seed-size faith is enough.

Regarding openness, I have seen a professing atheist receive the anointing. He told me that he was indeed open to the possibility that Jesus exists, but he had no faith it was so. He was simply open to be shown something — if it was true. He then received an impacting anointing, and dramatic fruits resulted.

The person receiving should be told that what he is sensing in the ministration is the effect of the Spirit of God upon his being. He has come to heal. The sick person must receive his healing in faith at that time.

The healing may be manifested immediately, or the healing may not be manifested immediately. The important thing is that the Spirit of the living God is upon the person. The anointing is present to heal.

The person must accept that God is serious and is not fooling. That one should then begin to express in words his thanks and praise for the healing he has received. He is to stand in this faith until the manifestation of the healing occurs.

The words that I have here presented regarding how to minister the Holy Spirit for healing are but expressions I use to bring forth the things in my heart regarding the Lord's instructions in John 7:37-39. Different words may express for others what is in their hearts, and they will, most assuredly, cause the anointing to flow. Words and concepts and experiences may differ from one to another. They are reflections of our past experiences. Use the words that best express your heart attitudes in the four matters the Lord calls for, and the anointing will flow.

In the following chapters, we will look at some of the many and various things the Holy Spirit anointing can be ministered to effect. He has come to us to express Himself in blessings — abundantly!

We have this treasure in jars of clay.   2 Corinthians 4:7

Let us learn to use our treasure lavishly.

Part II

FOR WHAT We May Minister the Anointing

CHAPTER 8

THE TREASURE WITHIN

We have this TREASURE in earthen vessels.   2 Corinthians 4:7, NKJ

This is the area around which the rest of the chapters of this book will be focused — the blessings that the Spirit is with us to manifest. The Treasure that is the Spirit of God in us brings forth treasures, as we minister the anointing to others.

First, let me state that when the Holy Spirit, God Almighty, comes to indwell a person, that person has come to the place for which he was created. Our Creator so fashioned us human beings that to function smoothly we need His indwelling presence. It is unto this state that our Savior has made possible restoration.

A person who is again privileged to be indwelt by divinity will have life and inner blessings that only this experience can bring. The consequences for all eternity will be enormous, for indeed God is with those whom He fills — always. God Himself is the greatest treasure a human being can ever have.

In this study, we are focusing upon the things that the Spirit comes to do in and through men and women in this present age. He has not come to us simply to make us feel good (although we give glory to God for the wondrous feelings and intimate sensings He manifests). He comes to us to do many things *in us,* and He comes to us to do many things *through us.* He works through us on behalf of others. He resides in believers with great purposes in mind to accomplish through us. In this sense, as a result of the indwelling Holy Spirit, we

79

have great treasure within us — all the things that the anointing will do in us and through us.

Now, a treasure is something that its possessor can use to provide for himself as needs and desires present themselves. When we have a natural treasure, we need not live in poverty, nor in lack of provision of any kind. And, having treasure allows us to bestow lavishly upon others. If a person has a natural treasure and he continues to live without needed food, shelter, clothing and other desirable things, he must be either ignorant of the presence of the treasure or ignorant of how to benefit from it. If not, he must be just plain stupid.

In this verse, Paul is saying by the Spirit: "You are a mortal being, with all the frailties and weaknesses of present-day humanity. But, having the Holy Spirit within you, you are a rich man. You have, in Him, a treasure — God Himself. Within you is God, ready, willing and well able to supply needed provisions to you and to others through you. So disposed is He to bless you with the use of His divine power that He has come personally to you, to dwell within you and to work through you." Wow! That's exciting.

Let us examine further this matter of the treasure we have, the Holy Spirit who lives in us to supply us with provision according to the will of God for our lives and for others. What does the Word of God teach regarding the supply that the Spirit has been given to me to furnish? What does the Word of God say that the Spirit does in and through those who have this treasure? Through ANYONE? What scriptures have been given to us that we might know God's will in this matter? What are the things He wills to do on behalf of the one in whom He resides? What things are revealed about the Holy Spirit that show us what He is like and how He desires to express Himself in this material world through the persons in whom He dwells?

There are more questions to be answered: What did the Holy Spirit do in and through the Lord Jesus, who then said that the same things He had done, and even greater things, would be done in and through His followers? Jesus said that He was going to His Father and that He would send the Spirit so that these things could be done.

What did the Holy Spirit do through other men in both the Old and the New Testaments? If we can learn the answer to these questions, we can know what we can have, for God makes no exception of persons. The things He has done through men and women of the Bible are the very things He desires to do through men and women today, including you and me.

This is a very personal message. I must learn the things that the Scriptures show are for me, for my own blessing and so that I can bless others. What things do I see the Holy Spirit doing as I take humble, exploratory steps into this awesome ministry? We believe that we are in the last few years before the Lord Jesus returns, and in the Word of God, we are promised the greatest outpouring of the Holy Spirit, the *"early and the latter rain,"* in our time (Joel 2:23). The Lord is telling many of His servants that the signs and wonders He will manifest in these years will be greater and greater as the time of His return nears.

ONE MORE GENERAL CONSIDERATION

Before we begin to focus on specific things for which we may minister the anointing, I believe it will be helpful to consider Holy Spirit ministry for supply as a matter of two broad general areas. The anointing may be ministered for what may be called either negative matters or positive matters. By "negative matters," I mean the Spirit's activity directed to matters or conditions I want removed or done away with. By "positive matters," I mean His activity directed to bring blessings or increase where needed.

There are areas and/or times in life when the supply we need requires the power of the Spirit to do away with things that are harmful or undesirable to us. These are problems or burdensome situations that we desire to have out of our lives because they are harmful to us or to others. The positive matters to which I refer are things we want or desire that are not presently with us, things of which we do not have an adequate supply. Therefore, we want these things, or we want more of them than we have at the time. We are seeking for increased blessing for ourselves and/or for others.

The Word of God teaches that the Treasure we have within us will give both of these kinds of treasures as we minister the anointing. The Holy Spirit will use His power to do away with negative things in the life of a believer. He will also use His power to bring positive blessings where needed.

NEGATIVE MATTERS

One promise with regard to negative matters is:

And it shall come to pass in that day, that his burden shall be taken away from off thy shoulder, and his yoke from off thy neck, and the yoke shall be destroyed because of the anointing.   Isaiah 10:27, KJV

This great Old Testament prophecy came to pass when the Jews were delivered from the Assyrians. Their deliverance came about because of the power of the Holy Spirit, the anointing. Under the Old Covenant, the anointing acted to deliver God's people from great burdens and oppressive yokes. In the New Testament (according to the book of Hebrews), we have a better covenant. The Holy Spirit continues to behave according to His nature and in accord with the will of God for His people. This will is always for deliverance from burdens and oppressions.

We have peace with God through our Lord Jesus Christ.   Romans 5:1

The source of burdens and oppressions has been defeated at the cross of Calvary. Now, the people of God are called to a victorious life because of that victory of the Lord Jesus. We are called to an overcoming life, not a life in which we are dominated by and subjugated to demonic burdens and oppressions.

We, now, have been given the Holy Spirit, the anointing. He is within us in order to be active in us and through us. This is how He will reveal what God is like.

Man was created to reveal the image and likeness of God. But it can only happen as God Himself is within man as the source of His own image and likeness. God wants to be flowing forth from men in the earth. He wants to express Himself through them in their behavior and in their deeds. He wants to do His works through men. Thus, He will reveal in creation just what He is like. This is the way the knowledge of the glory of God is meant to fill the earth, even as the waters cover the sea.

In this present age, God is a burden lifter. He is a yoke destroyer. By His Spirit, He will act, as men minister the anointing. I have seen the anointing lift countless burdens and destroy many, many yokes!

Isaiah 10:27 speaks of the negative matters that the Holy Spirit will take out of the life of a believer. In the wide and rich salvation that the shed blood of the Lord has procured, this is Good News. Paul calls this the Gospel of peace, the Good News of peace (see Romans 5:1 and Ephesians 6:15).

God wills to be at peace with any man once that man is reconciled to Him through the shed blood of His provided Sacrificial Lamb, the Anointed Jesus. After this happens, His will for His born-again children is that they have peace in His creation. The onerous consequences of sin, evil oppressions of all sorts, are not God's will for those who are at peace with the Creator.

It remains a harsh reality that evil is still working to place burdens on men until the Lord returns. Thus, evil forces, evil consequences, or what I am here calling negative matters, still attack God's children. To deal with these negative matters, the Holy Spirit, the anointing, has been given. He will work in us, for the good of our own lives, and through us on behalf of others, to lift the burdens and to destroy the oppressions.

The descriptive words of the Scriptures "burdens" and "yokes [oppressions]" are broad terms that cover a multitude of negative matters. Many of the things that trouble our lives can be grouped under these words. Yet, for the elimination of all such things from the lives of men, the Holy Spirit is available. What wonderful, wonderful Good News! What a great Gospel of peace!

The "burdens," or oppressions, that can afflict us include sickness, poverty, mental weaknesses, emotional problems, volitional weakness, disasters of all sorts, tragedies, difficult conditions, oppression by other people, oppression by spirit forces, etc. When these are present in our lives, they bring heavy weights with them. If they last, the oppressed person becomes sorely burdened. The power of the anointing is available to lift us out of such oppressions and to destroy them.

The Word of God proclaims, in Romans 8, that we are more than conquerors through Christ — that is, through the Anointed One, the One with the anointing of the Spirit, the One who has given to us the same Spirit anointing. This may seem to others like a very hollow boast if we accept a life of burdens and oppressions.

Being free from oppression does not become a reality just because we say it. Christians, as do all men, want to live free from burdens and oppressions, but coming into a victorious life such as this requires the divine power of the anointing. Recourse to the anointing must be taken, therefore, whenever negative matters present themselves. We have the Treasure of the Spirit within us, and He is ready to give to us the treasures we need in this regard.

How many burdened and oppressed believers are there who through ignorance or unbelief are not ministering the anointing against negative matters? Surely the number would be many millions, for under this great umbrella, "burdens" and "oppressions," there fall many weights.

When a negative matter comes into your life, it should be identified immediately for what it is, a burden and/or an oppression. You should be convinced that the will of God is against such things. Then, you should begin to minister the anointing to do that for which He has come to live in you to do. Start to use the Treasure you have in you. He will bring you the provision or alleviation you need.

POSITIVE MATTERS

Just eight verses after the *"in that day"* of Isaiah 10:27, the Holy Spirit focuses full upon the time of the coming Anointed One, the Messiah. In 10:27, the Spirit began to contemplate deliverance from evil for the people of God. As we read on to Isaiah 11:1, we see that the Spirit comes to the future appearance of the Messiah. Yes, by the anointing, the Messiah would bring deliverance from burdens and from other consequences of evil. But, there is more! In 11:1 is proclaimed the wondrous Good News that the anointing would also bring positive blessings. Isaiah says that the anointing in Messiah would act in Him for wisdom, understanding, counsel, power, etc. Divine increase of such things would come to Messiah by the Spirit of God. Through His anointing, He would have these things which were not natural to a human being.

Philippians 2:6-8 reveals that the Lord Jesus chose to come to earth, where He would live as a human being, totally subject to human limitations and weaknesses in all things. (The only exception would be that He was without sin.) He purposely did not employ His own divine attributes as He worked out salvation for the human race. In His lifetime, things of the divine nature were worked out through Him by the anointing of the Holy Spirit.

When we come to Isaiah 11:9, we learn of God's overall purpose regarding His creation: "... *for the earth will be full of the knowledge of the* LORD *as the waters cover the sea."* This will be worked out through millions of men and women, as the fruits of the anointing are shown forth through them. They will minister the anointing everywhere on the earth! The same Holy Spirit who anointed Jesus has been given to us for similar activity now.

Just as a simple example, only yesterday I was faced with a rather common matter that required a decision on my part. I was perplexed regarding the best way to handle the matter to insure my greatest profit. I had to face my lack of wisdom concerning that issue.

Before I went to sleep last night, I again analyzed the matter before the Lord. I admitted my lack of wisdom in the matter. Then I ministered the anointing to myself, in order that the Spirit of wisdom manifest Himself to me in this regard. I thanked the Lord and went to sleep.

When I awoke this morning and turned to the Lord, the knot that the matter had created in me began to unravel and I saw clearly the action to take. I also saw what was to be avoided. Having decided what action to take, I felt the peace of God fill me. The Spirit of wisdom had enlightened my befuddled thinking. The Treasure within me had given me the supply and the provision I had lacked. In the process, I learned more about what God was like. His great goodness and His personal interest in me were revealed.

In Luke 4:18-19, there is set forth the role of the anointing regarding lifting certain burdens and oppressions — and *also* to give positive provisions. After the Lord said, in verse 18, that the anointing had come upon Him to do away with certain negative matters (poverty, sicknesses and demonic captivity and oppression — things that Isaiah 10:27 also refers to), He said, in verse 19, that the Spirit would act to produce positive things. He spoke of the blessings of increase and of abundance that the anointing was upon Him to manifest. And He said that this Good News was to be spread abroad publicly!

"The Spirit of the Lord is on me, because he has anointed me ... TO PRO-CLAIM THE YEAR OF THE LORD'S FAVOR."   Luke 4:18-19

"The year of the Lord's favor" refers to the Year of the Jubilee. In Old Testament days, the Lord provided unique blessings to Israel throughout an entire year every fiftieth year. It was called the Year of Jubilee. This was a year in which extraordinary blessings were received by the people of God — physical blessings such as rest from their labors and economic blessings. The Amplified Version of the Bible translates this phrase as *"the day when salvation and the free favors of God profusely abound."*

The Lord is speaking here of the wonders that He had come to earth to bring to mankind. He came to bring life, the very divine life of God, and He came to bring that life more abundantly than it had ever been available to man before. Life, in its many aspects, was to be expressed in and through the Lord Jesus Christ by the anointing that had come upon Him.

In verses 18 and 19, the Lord said that the Holy Spirit anointing had been given to Him to do these things: to counteract negative things, things that are burdens and oppressions to men, *and* to bestow positive blessings upon men as they are needed. He was saying that it was to do these things that the anointing of the Spirit had come upon Him. And it happened while He was living as a man.

This is the same Holy Spirit anointing that comes upon ANYONE and EVERYONE in whom He resides permanently, those who are baptized with the Holy Spirit. He has been given to them by the Lord

Jesus to do what the Lord said the anointing did through Him. He said that the same things He did by the anointing, and even greater things than the anointing did through Him, would be done by His followers.

When I first began to see this concept — the Holy Spirit manifested to do wondrous things through me as He had through the Lord Jesus — I found that I was fearful of even considering such an idea. What colossal presumption it seemed to me at the time!

Then the awesome concept kept on cropping up, even as I tried to push it from me as an unholy thought. Gradually I began to deal with it. At first, I only gingerly analyzed it, looking to the Holy Spirit for assurance and for guidance. Finally, I came to a clear understanding of what the Word of God teaches. Although the thought still inspired fear and trembling in me, I began to accept it.

Then I was faced with the challenge of acting upon what I had seen, of ministering the anointing, and allowing it to flow from me to do the things that the Spirit did through the Lord Jesus. As I tiptoed into this new spiritual ground, what delightful discoveries awaited me! In instance after instance, it became clear that the Scriptures were teaching just that. It has now been more than seven years since I began ministering the anointing to lift burdens and to give positive blessings — to myself and to others, and the experience only grows sweeter.

Some readers may doubt what I am saying. Their theology or tradition, or even their sincere opinions of scriptural teaching may cause them to rebel against these claims. I can personally assure you that the anointing flows from me in a wondrous way to do these things. I have been in five different countries in the past seven years and have ministered in more than one hundred and eighty churches and in hundreds of homes. I have ministered the anointing in countless ordinary situations of daily living. Always, when I minister the anointing according to the teaching of the Lord in John 7:37-39, the Holy Spirit flows with power to do the things for which I am ministering His power.

I make no claim nor pretense to any unique gift from God. The gift that I have from God is the gift of the Holy Spirit spoken of in John 4, the promise of God spoken of in the book of Acts. This is the gift of God offered to every believer. It is the gift that comes to ANYONE who is baptized in the Spirit by the Lord Jesus.

I have taught these simple principles of John 7:37-39 to many tens of thousands of people, and the same results occur through them as through me.

There is only one Holy Spirit. He is the same divine person in a child of ten years of age as in an adult of seventy years. He is the same divine person in a credentialed, ordained minister as He is in a so-called lay person.

The Spirit may have been in one person for fifty years, and He may have been in another for only ten minutes. But where He resides, He has come to flow out in power to lift burdens and to bring blessings. Anyone who has received the Holy Spirit and who begins to act in faith on John 7:37-39 will immediately begin to see the anointing manifested. Burdens will lift, and blessings will come.

Do you have this Treasure in you through the baptism of the Holy Spirit? If so, begin to minister the anointing to yourself or to others — even as Peter did in Acts 3. He said, *"What I have I give you."* He was speaking of the anointing of the Spirit for the supply needed.

If you do not yet have this Treasure within you, find someone who does and who knows how to minister the Spirit to others.

Now, in the succeeding chapters, let us look at some of the burdens and oppressions that the Holy Spirit will lift as you minister the anointing. Let us also look at some of the many, many blessings for which the anointing will flow forth from you.

CHAPTER 9

HE HAS ANOINTED ME TO DO THINGS

"The Spirit of the LORD is upon Me,
Because He has anointed Me to preach the gospel to the poor;
He has sent Me to heal the brokenhearted,
To proclaim liberty to the captives
And recovery of sight to the blind,
To set at liberty those who are oppressed;
To proclaim the acceptable year of the LORD."   Luke 4:18-19, NKJ

These are clearly things that we may minister through the anointing. Jesus here places an emphasis on the Holy Spirit doing definite works, for it was to do certain things that the anointing has been given.

Being Almighty God, the Holy Spirit can and does manifest Himself in the physical world as He pleases, according to His sovereign will. These manifestations result in many and differing consequences.

In Genesis 1:3, we learn of His initial sovereign workings in creation as we know it today. We see Him in His role in the formation of the natural world.

As the Old Testament continues on, the reported manifestations of the Spirit are many. Some were sovereign on His part, as the miracle birth of Isaac to Sarah in her old age or the occasional appearances of God to men.

Sometimes the Spirit's work, however, resulted through the agency of men such as Moses, Elijah, Elisha, Samson and David. These and others like them were often agents of the activities of the anointing.

Let us take careful note of the way the Spirit behaved with these agents of the anointing. Although He resided permanently in no one after He left Adam, He still *"came upon"* a certain few — mostly prophets, kings and priests — to do the works of their callings. The anointing lifted from them after the work was done, for none was His permanent abode.

It was not until the Holy Spirit came upon Jesus of Nazareth that He (the Spirit) again took up permanent residence in a human being. When the anointing came upon Jesus, it made Him the Messiah, so that He was now doing things He had not been able to do before. And, this, He said very clearly, was the purpose of the coming of the Holy Spirit — to do things. Then He went on to list a few of the things the Spirit had come to do.

After He was glorified, the Lord Jesus began to give this same Holy Spirit to other men so that the anointing could continue doing the things the Holy Spirit was sent to the earth to do.

One such thing was to fill a person with the sensing of the presence of Jesus, a most important matter. But this was, in no way, the only thing the Spirit was sent to do. We, as believers, have become members of the Body of Christ (the Anointed One). The Head of the Body, the Anointed One, intends that the same anointing He had be expressed through each member of His Body to perform works, to do the many things the Holy Spirit is within us to do.

There are wonderful feelings and sublime sensations that the anointing gives to those in whom He dwells, and we should participate in these spiritual delights. But we must not be content only with such participations (as has been the case with far too many Christians). In the wonderment of having the anointing manifest the presence of God in us, it is a great mistake not to look further into the Word of God and learn of all the many other things the Spirit has come to do through each believer .

As we have seen, one of the things the anointing has come to do as He resides in us is to lift burdens and destroy oppressions (see Isaiah 10:27). In Luke 4:18-19, the Lord listed five burdens that the Holy Spirit came upon Him to lift. The same Holy Spirit anointing is now upon every believer baptized in the Spirit, to do those same things. What are some of those things?

He Has Anointed Me to Do Things

THE SPIRIT OF THE LORD IS UPON ME, BECAUSE HE HAS ANOINTED ME TO PREACH THE GOSPEL TO THE POOR

For many years, as a Roman Catholic, I accepted what I had been taught by my religious leaders regarding this phrase. They taught that this means Jesus came to preach salvation and the Word of God to the poor, to the destitute, to those without material blessings in this world. Behind this teaching is the belief that God has a unique love for people in poverty. The idea is that poverty and separation from material blessings are agents to bring one to holiness. God is pleased when they hold dominion over people. He loves those who are poor, and He loves to keep them in their poverty. Spiritual betterment surely will result from their hard economic conditions.

I embraced these teachings by taking a vow of poverty as a member of a religious order. We were assured that God greatly loves those of His servants who live a life of poverty. Poverty was a sure road to sanctity. This verse in Luke 4 was held out as evidence for this view.

"Did not Jesus come to bring salvation to the poor?" we were asked. And we were reminded of Saint X and Saint Y, who had embraced holy poverty. In their poverty, they were models of how followers of Jesus should live. If we were poor, God would love us greatly for it, and if we stayed poor, we would grow in holiness.

This thinking and the practice of poverty it produced influenced me deeply for many years. In the end, I needed a great washing of my spirit and of my mind by the Word of God before I could see how erroneous the teaching really was. What great burdens result to a man because of this teaching — both physical burdens and spiritual burdens. I needed deliverance from the spirit of poverty, which had come about because I had embraced wholly a belief contrary to the Word of God.

The Word of God is clear to anyone who is open to hear it, and it teaches that poverty is a curse, that it is not, in any way, a blessing. Poverty is a burden, an oppressive burden, for all men.

God Himself is the richest of living beings, and He is a lavish Father to those who belong to Him. What rich father could look with delight upon a beloved child living in oppressive poverty? That the infinitely good and powerful God desires poverty in His children is absurd. The concept is against reason and against the teachings of the Scriptures.

Poverty is a burden. And there are demon spirits of poverty at work to lay this oppression upon as many humans as possible. The Holy Spirit was upon the Lord Jesus to proclaim the Good News to the poor, and the Good News He brought was this: "Poor, you do not have to be poor any longer! Poor, the anointing has come to lift the burden of poverty that is breaking your financial back! Poor, the Holy Spirit is now available to save you from poverty!"

It is not the purpose of this book to deal at length with the biblical teachings on the blessings of prosperity that are God's will for His people. Nor is this the place to enter into consideration of the important place of tithing and giving that brings forth God's material blessings. There are many wonderful books and tapes available on this subject. I am focusing on the power of the anointing to lift burdens, among them, the burden of poverty.

In many cases, as in mine, deliverance by the power of the Spirit from demons of poverty is needed. (I will deal with deliverance later in this chapter.) Then, there is the matter of existing debts. The anointing may also be ministered to bring one to a debt-free status. And, finally, there is the matter of the needed increase in financial blessings afterwards — the increase that will bring a person into the blessing of financial prosperity.

Freedom from debt and an increase in prosperity is clearly one of the reasons for which the anointing has been given. It remains for the people of God to minister the anointing within themselves to receive the material blessings their Father in Heaven wills for them.

After I had received deliverance from spirits of poverty, and they lifted from me, from my life and from my circumstances, I then began to tithe and to give offerings in faith in the promises of the Word of God. I also learned to minister the anointing, the Spirit of prosperity, to my life. The anointing comes upon me to do things that lead to prosperity in my daily living, and I minister the Spirit of prosperity to myself frequently. The result is that I am enjoying God's will for material prosperity in my life.

He Has Anointed Me to Do Things

When I teach seminars on the anointing, I include these truths and lead others into these things. When I do, the Spirit always flows, and beautiful material blessings result.

Here is an example of the way one may minister the Spirit of prosperity to himself or to others:

Lord Jesus,

I thirst for prosperity. I sincerely desire it.
I now seek Your precious presence, Lord.
I drink of You, Lord, spirit-to-Spirit.
And I believe that You are doing what You say. You are having the anointing
flow from me for prosperity (debt removal, increase, etc.).

Then I boldly speak out my faith:

In Your name, Lord, the Spirit of prosperity is now upon me and flowing to
effect these things.

As time passes, during which time the Spirit works out these blessings in us, we must keep bathing our minds in the words that assure us of God's will regarding prosperity. Note that Philippians 4:19 teaches that these things will come to pass through Christ Jesus, that is, through the Anointed One. It is because He has given the same anointing of the Spirit to us that our needs may be supplied through the working of the Spirit in His power.

THE SPIRIT OF THE LORD IS UPON ME, BECAUSE HE HAS ANOINTED ME ... HE HAS SENT ME TO HEAL THE BROKENHEARTED, [TO PREACH] RECOVERY OF SIGHT TO THE BLIND

The anointing has been given to lift burdens that are upon men (see Isaiah 10:27). In these portions of our text, the Lord continues dealing with the negative things that the Spirit will lift from humans. He says that the anointing will act to bring healing — healing within a person's soul (mind, emotions and will), and physical healings. The negative things that afflict men, sicknesses of all sorts, are presented as matters for elimination by the Spirit that had come upon Jesus. During His life on earth, the Lord faithfully complied with this purpose for which the anointing had come upon Him. The Scriptures say of Him:

How God anointed Jesus of Nazareth with the Holy Spirit and with power, who went about DOING GOOD and HEALING all who were oppressed by the devil, for God was with Him.   Acts 10:38, NKJ

He was *"doing good"* — bringing positive blessings of increase to men everywhere He met them. He was "healing" — destroying sicknesses and other negative things that the forces of evil had laid upon men. This is the same Spirit of God, the same anointing, that is upon me (see 1 John 2:20). This is the same anointing that remains in me (see 1 John 2:27). This is the same anointing that has come to reside in everyone who has received the baptism of the Holy Spirit.

In John 7:37-39, the Lord Jesus teaches the four steps one's heart must take in order that the anointing flow out in power (in this case, power to heal). These should be done by one who wishes to minister the anointing.

How Best to Receive the Anointing

What about the person who needs to receive the anointing? How does one receive what the Holy Spirit has come to impart? What should be happening within the person who is seeking healing by the impartation of the anointing?

We have seen that the person ministering the anointing is doing so with the DESIRE that the person receiving the anointing be healed. The minister has come into the PRESENCE OF THE LORD for this. The minister's thirst and compassion and love are at work, as he seeks healing for the one in need. The minister is DRINKING of the Lord for this. The minister is using his FAITH in the words of the Lord that the anointing will now flow forth. This is all well and good, but it behooves the one who would receive the blessing to know just how to

94

receive. Optimum results come from optimum attitudes and activity, both on the part of the one who is ministering and on the part of the one who is receiving.

The Word of God gives the answer to the question of how to receive the anointing. There is a remarkable story of the flow of the anointing to heal a sickness, remarkable in that it proclaims loudly the great desire of the Holy Spirit to fulfill His charge to heal men. Also, it is remarkable in what it reveals regarding how one best receives the anointing for healing (or for other matters). It is profitable to analyze what was going on within the woman who was healed in this account in Mark 5:21-34:

1. The woman had a great DESIRE for her healing. In the words of the Lord, she was THIRSTING after it. She had been sick for twelve years. Her healing had long been her goal. She had placed it as the number one priority of her life. She had sought medical help everywhere — going to many doctors and taking treatments of every sort. To pay the expenses to obtain her number one desire, she had sold her house, her furniture, her clothing, her animals, all her possessions — everything she had. Still, when she came to Jesus, she was in worse physical condition than ever. She was still seeking her healing.
This woman was so THIRSTY for her healing that no matter what she had spent in vain, no matter what the frustrations of the past had been, no matter how many healers had failed her, she still wanted her healing more than anything.
The woman demonstrated her great singleness of purpose. Hearing the Word of God that was going around the neighborhood (Luke 4:18-19 and Acts 10:38), she accepted it. She took it to herself in faith and acted upon it. So great was her thirst.

2. The woman sought out the PRESENCE OF THE LORD JESUS with great determination. Finding herself in the center of a great multitude and with many people pressing in all around her to see Jesus, she determined to reach Him too.
The crowd was moving slowly toward the house of Jairus, one

of the Jewish religious leaders, where Jesus intended to perform an important ministry mission. The others were moving with Him.

I have never seen a crowd of people that did not have in it many in need of healing. I have asked in both large and small gatherings, and many hands always go up to indicate their need for it. Often, more than fifty percent of the people are sick. In a large multitude, such as was with the Lord that day, there must have been many in such need. Yet, as this sickly woman came to Him, He was not ministering healing to the other people, and none of them were asking for it. They were not doing anything about their own needs. They were just passively following after Jesus as He made His way to the house of Jairus.

Then, this woman somehow made her way through the multitude to where Jesus was. She was filled with just one thing, her great desire for her healing. For this, she sought the presence of Jesus. One can easily imagine the silent cry of her heart: "I want my healing! I don't care where He is going or what He is doing, I want my healing! I don't care if no one else is being healed. I want mine! I don't care if no one here receives anything from Him. I must have my healing now!" And so she sought the presence of the Lord Jesus, with great singleness of purpose.

3. The woman knew that Jesus had the anointing of the Holy Spirit of God. She centered her needs and wants in Him, fully intending to draw from Him the healing power of the Spirit. She came to Him in dependence for the provision she needed. She came to Him as the Source of the flow of the anointing.

One may say, in the Lord's metaphor of John 7:37-38, she had come to DRINK OF THE LORD JESUS. For from Him there would flow to her the anointing for healing.

What simple reasoning she employed: *"If I but touch His clothes, I shall be whole."* She reasoned that the anointing that had been flowing out from Him must necessarily pass through His clothes. The anointing must first "drench" His clothing as it passes out from Him to others. Surely, she reasoned with child-like faith, there is enough of the anointing left in His clothing to heal me, if I but touch it.

(I have often wondered if perhaps this incident was the grounds upon which Paul developed his practice of imparting cloths with the anointing for healing [see Acts 19]. At any rate, I have experienced that ANYONE today may do the same as Paul did, impart the anointing for healing to a cloth. The anointing will then flow to a sick person when the cloth is later laid upon him.)

4. The woman BELIEVED, and acting on her faith, she caused the anointing to flow to herself. She believed the word she had heard regarding the Lord Jesus. She believed that the anointing for healing would flow to her as she drew from Jesus, the Source of the anointing.

The anointing flowed to this woman under conditions that must cause us to marvel. Up to the moment of the flow of the anointing, Jesus was not even aware of her existence, let alone of her need for healing. He was in no way cooperating with her for the flow of the anointing for her healing. He was intent on reaching the house of Jairus, as He walked along with the slowly-moving throng. He was being pressed and pushed from all sides as He walked.

Still, once this woman had done what she had purposed, once the Holy Spirit had flowed out from Him, Jesus immediately knew what had happened. Woosh! He had felt the outflowing anointing. The Spirit had come forth from Him in power.

There is an unmistakable sensing of this on the part of the person who ministers the Holy Spirit. Such a marvelous occurrence! There is a filling up within one with the anointing, as the Spirit rises up to act through him. And then there comes a release, sometimes soft, sometimes explosive, as the Spirit goes forth to act.

I know this glorious experience that the Lord Jesus was sensing, for I have experienced it thousands of times. I have also seen tens of thousands of other believers experience the same thing, as they, too, have ministered the anointing in power to others.

Let us take special note that what happened in this account is a precious revelation regarding the will of God to heal the sick, for the anointing has come to men to heal the sick. The Lord was not even aware of the woman's illness when she came to drink of Him. She did not even ask Him to minister the anointing to her. In fact, He didn't. It was all the doing of the Holy Spirit.

God Almighty, present in the man Jesus, was acutely aware of what was going on within this woman as she drew near to the Lord. As the woman did all she could to draw near to the Lord, the Spirit of God in Jesus saw:

a) Her great THIRST for healing.

b) Her COMING INTO THE PRESENCE OF THE LORD JESUS.

c) Her dependence on the Lord Jesus as the Source of the flow of the anointing — her drinking of the Lord Jesus.

d) Her FAITH in the Word of God and in the Lord Jesus that the anointing would heal her.

Since the Spirit was in the Lord Jesus to lift the burden of sicknesses, upon seeing these aspects of her heart, the anointing flowed out sovereignly on the part of God!

Some still ask, "Does God will to heal the sick?" This story is compelling evidence that He does.

This woman did not come asking, nor praying for healing by the anointing. She came taking what she knew was hers according to the heart of God. She knew in her heart the principle expressed by the writer of Hebrews:

Let us therefore come BOLDLY unto the throne of grace, that we may obtain mercy, and find grace to help in time of need.   Hebrews 4:16, KJV

The woman had come to Jesus with great boldness, ignoring the hundreds of people who thronged Him. She took, boldly, the grace of healing by the anointing, and Jesus marveled at her. He was astonished to find a person with such great faith as hers. It was unique in His time, just as it is today.

When I read the words of Jesus in verse 34, I get the sense that He was saying, "Woman, you have just made My day because of your faith and your understanding of the anointing! Wow! You're healed, and you will stay healed!"

Again, this woman received healing by the anointing as she:

a) THIRSTED for healing.
b) CAME INTO THE PRESENCE OF THE LORD JESUS for healing by the anointing.
c) Drew from Him (or DRANK OF HIM).
d) BELIEVED ON HIM, spoke words of faith and acted upon them.

She RECEIVED the anointing and its blessing as she did exactly what the Lord teaches ANYONE to do who would minister the anointing to others.

Let me testify that the Lord Jesus and the Holy Spirit are the same today as on that day in Mark 5, and the anointing today is still able to heal. Some months ago I was teaching a seminar on the anointing to a group of a hundred or so people in a church in Bogota, Colombia. After the teaching, I began laying hands on the people one by one for the provisions they needed through the anointing. All the people were falling down under the power of the Spirit as I ministered to them. (On some days, no one falls down. On other days, a few fall. And on other days, many fall or even all fall. But always the anointing flows! It isn't either the falling or the lack of falling that counts. It is the flow of the anointing that matters, the bathing of the one seeking the anointing.)

That particular day, Jorge Fresneda, a friend of mine, was standing behind each person I ministered to, catching him (or her) as he fell under the power. One by one, Jorge served everyone in the meeting in this manner. Then, as I was finishing with the last person who had been in the teaching, Jorge smiled at me, saying, "And me, Albert? The anointing for my need?"

"Of course," I said to my friend, and I began to lift my right hand to place it on his head. But before I could touch him and before I could say any words of ministry, I felt someone on my right side grabbing my arm roughly.

There was a loud cry from a man at my side, " I want my healing! I want my healing! Look, my hand is paralyzed!" I felt annoyance at this rude intrusion, for I had been focusing on Jorge and his need. The other man was jarring me from my concentration.

Still, I didn't look at the person annoying me. I kept on looking at Jorge, and I spoke out of the corner of my mouth at the intruder: "Just a minute, brother. Let me finish with Jorge. Then it will be your turn."

But the man would not let go of my arm. He cried out even louder: "I want my healing! I want my healing, now! My hand is paralyzed!"

I looked again at Jorge and shrugged. "Just a minute, Jorge," I offered, and I turned to look at the source of this annoying interruption. A man had his left hand on my right arm. Extended high above us was his right arm, its hand and fingers frozen in the form of a claw.

Then, suddenly, his fingers began to move. "Look," he screamed, "I am healed! My fingers are moving!" Over and over he continued to scream, "I'm healed! I'm healed! I'm healed!" Overcome with emotion, he fell to the ground. Later, after he had calmed down somewhat, he explained to us what had happened.

The man had been a worker in a factory in the city of Cali and had suffered an industrial accident. The tendons of his right arm had been severed. His hand and fingers could not move. They were paralyzed.

He told us that in Cali he had gone from hospital to hospital, clinic to clinic, doctor to doctor, seeking help. He had spent every peso he had in his efforts to recover, and was forced to sell every possession he had to pay the bills. He had absolutely no material resources left, but still there was no one who could help him.

He had thirsted intensely after his healing. One day it came to him that surely there were better medical specialists in the capital city. He must go to Bogota. He had not a single peso in his pocket, but he nevertheless set out to walk the more than four hundred and fifty kilometers between the two cities. It is not a journey over flat ground. There are two deep valleys and two high mountains to cross. The final ascent to the plains of Bogota at nine thousand feet is long and arduous.

He Has Anointed Me to Do Things

There was extreme cold at the peaks, one of them sitting twelve thousand feet high, and there was tropical heat in the valleys. But nothing mattered to this man. He could only think of his great desire for healing. All the frustrations of failure he had experienced in Cali did not deter him.

He admitted that during the five weeks it took him to walk the distance to the capital, he had been forced to steal in order to live — a chicken here, an egg there, fruit or vegetables in the field — whatever he could find in the farms along the way. He had been sleeping with animals and he had not washed even once (Believe me, it was evident!).

He finally reached Bogota, and that morning he was walking past the church where I was ministering the anointing. He heard that there was a man within, ministering the Holy Spirit for healing. He believed that the Lord Jesus wanted to heal him. He entered the building and pushed his way through the people around me. And, in his great desire, He drew to himself the anointing for healing. The anointing flowed to that man. He was healed instantly, and remains so to this day.

When the anointing flowed from me to him, I was not even aware of his existence, much less of his need for healing. I was not even looking at him when the anointing began to flow to him. In no way was I consciously ministering the anointing to him.

Still, the Spirit of God was acutely in touch with all that was going on within that man's heart. He was in perfect heart disposition to receive the anointing. He would not be denied, and the anointing flowed for his healing.

The Holy Spirit is the same today as He was at the time of the incident recorded in Mark 5. With this man, the Spirit behaved the same as He had with the woman who sought healing from Jesus. It happened because this man's heart was expressing the same things toward God as the woman had expressed. The anointing poured forth due to their heart attitudes. This is one of the reasons I try to explain to a person about to receive the anointing, the best way to do so. I know that it works.

The works of Jesus, the Anointed One, are truly being done through men. They are the same works as were done through Him, just as He said would happen (see John 14:12-14). Jesus has gone to be with the Father, and from there He now baptizes with the Holy Spirit ANY-ONE who wants. By the same Spirit, the Lord continues doing His works through the yielded members of His Body.

I find it very helpful to someone seeking the anointing, to take him through the four heart attitudes that the woman in Mark 5 expressed, the heart attitudes that caused the Holy Spirit to so impulsively flow out to her in power. I find that if I take the time to prepare a person in this way to receive, the flow readily gushes forth.

Also, I find it delightful when persons come to me for ministry with these heart attitudes already present in them. Many times, the anointing begins to flow from me before I begin to minister to these people. As I then center my own heart attitudes properly, the flow becomes very great. There are times when I sense the going forth of the anointing so strongly that it seems that all my insides are flowing out with it. Dramatic things result.

In March of 1999, I witnessed something striking in a small town in Colombia. It happened to dozens of people, some of them just new to the things of the Lord and His Spirit. After the people had learned the principles of John 7:37-39, individually they began to minister the anointing to others for healing. As they did this, they began to sense a tremendous gushing forth of the Spirit from within. They told me that with the great pouring forth they felt, it seemed that their chests and stomachs were bursting outward. They each lost their strength to stand and eventually collapsed onto the floor and lay there unconscious.

When the people came to their senses, they still lay on the floor, exhausted and groggy. Each had to be physically aided to stand again, and to be helped to the next person awaiting ministry. Then, each became fully lucid, completely possessed of his natural strengths, and eager to minister again. This scenario was then repeated again. And it happened over and over and over again for about an hour. When each of them had finally finished ministering to many people, they marveled at the wonders and delights they had been experiencing. Each person ministering the anointing had been completely overcome and had fallen under the power as he ministered it.

This causes me to wonder. For decades now, we have had the practice of using "catchers," those who stand behind the ones receiving the ministry of the anointing and aiding them as they fall to the floor. With these new ministerings, we needed "catchers" on both sides — one for the minister and one for the person receiving the ministry of the anointing. I wonder what other new things are at hand, and in what other new ways we will be blessed by the Spirit in the days ahead. The Lord is in the process of taking us to new dimensions of Holy Spirit ministry.

In this case in Colombia, the Lord was working with unusually great power through "nobodies." They were new believers, with no fame whatsoever as Holy Spirit ministers. He was doing His work with ANYONE, as He said He would in John 7:37-39.

THE SPIRIT OF THE LORD IS UPON ME, BECAUSE HE HAS ANOINTED ME ... HE HAS SENT ME TO HEAL THE BROKENHEARTED

In this portion of Luke 4:18, the Lord Jesus proclaims that the anointing of the Holy Spirit has been given (to Him, and then by Him to ANYONE who complies with His instructions), not only for physical healing, but also for interior, or inner, healing. The Holy Spirit can heal suffering minds, aching hearts, wounds in the emotions and broken hearts. Some people have interior burdens that are causing them as much grief as their physical sicknesses. There have been deep scars worked into their inner beings that keep them from healthy personality behavior. Their minds, emotions and wills are truly sick. They carry heavy, inner burdens that constantly oppress them.

Here is a partial list of some of the causes of these needs for inner healing, and for which the anointing is waiting to be ministered for healing:

- Abandonment by parents
- Rejection and/or lack of love from parents
- Rejection by a loved one or spouse
- Divorce
- Abuse of any kind by others
- Maltreatment by others, or by circumstances in life, even if done many years in the past

• Harsh circumstances of birth or environment that have resulted in personal deprivation (These may be actual or imagined.)

The list could go on and on. There are many adverse happenings in life that leave deep, permanent, inner scars. People are flocking to psychiatrists and counselors, desperate for help. The Lord Jesus has sent the Holy Spirit to us to heal such things.

We are to minister the anointing for the healing of such inner conditions. Some of the most dramatic healings and subsequent transformations I have seen have come after ministering the anointing to heal the brokenhearted. Instant healings abound in such ministry.

I find that such ministry is of great value to the person in need when I take time to personally draw upon the Lord Jesus to express His heart of compassion through me. In these cases, I need to speak with heartfelt sincerity and genuine affection and with love engendered by the Spirit of love. I need to throw myself wholly into the service, and when I do, I see the anointing flow forth doing wonders for such needy people.

THE SPIRIT OF THE LORD IS UPON ME, BECAUSE HE HAS ANOINTED ME ... TO PREACH DELIVERANCE TO THE CAPTIVES

This portion of Luke 4:18 speaks directly to the great source of burdens that the anointing has been given to lift from men. It deals with deliverance for people who are in bondage to demon spirits.

Again, let me underline the purpose of this book. It is to call all believers to a continual habit of ministering the anointing of the Holy Spirit to do the power works He has been sent to do through us. I want to explain how simple this is as one believes and acts in faith on the words of the Lord in John 7:37-39. And I want to point out some of the many things the anointing will do through any such person.

Therefore, I do not wish, at this point, to be sidetracked into disputes of who can or who cannot be influenced or dominated by demon spirits. Many studies presently exist on this subject. For me, it is not so much a matter of theological correctness as it is one of practical need. People are greatly distressed because of demon activity, far more than is under-

stood or accepted. My beliefs and my ministry behavior in this matter
have been influenced by the personal need for deliverance I myself had.
What unspeakable blessings resulted to me afterward! How can I not
offer to others this great treasure that deliverance by the Holy Spirit can
be for them?

In the seminars on the anointing that I have been teaching, I present
the matter of deliverance to the people in this manner: "Brothers and
sisters — all of you here — I am in no way judging any one of you regarding whether there are demons influencing you or active in your
life. But the facts of life are these:

- Demons of poverty are at work in the lives of individuals and in
  nations.
- Demons of ungodly behavior cause compulsive behaviors (un-
  forgiveness, irritation, bitterness, unholy sexual behavior, anger,
  resentments, depression, hatred, etc.) in many people — believers and nonbelievers alike.
- Demons of the occult work in the lives of many people, some as a
  result of occult practices that they have engaged in, others due to
  occult activity on the part of their ancestors.
- Demons of infirmity and of sickness are at work in many people.
  Sometimes they are present for many years before they manifest
  the illnesses.
- There are at work demons of divorce, of abortion, of ruin of all
  sorts.

"Truly, the list is a long one. Brothers, sisters, we humans open the
door to our lives, giving access to demons to influence us, especially
with regard to sinful habits of the past. I'm asking you now to present
yourself humbly before the Lord Jesus, for HIM, not me, to search your
life — should there be any demonic activity present with you. Would
it not be prudent and of possibly great advantage to you to so humble
yourself before Him? Why would you not want to cry to Him from
your heart, 'Lord Jesus, in case You find any demonic influences in my
life, I want deliverance by Your Spirit?' "

In this manner, I have offered deliverance, at times to a single person and at other times to several or to several hundred people at the same time. They most generally accept this invitation. I think it helps them to know that I will not name the demons present in them if there are any. The Lord has shown me to minister the anointing for deliverance without naming the demons. In this way, people are assured that their "dirty laundry" will not be aired publicly.

I do it in the following way: I have all the people remain seated. Then, I say to them words like these: "In the name of Jesus, the anointing comes upon you to deliver you from the influence of any and every demon at work in your life ... right now!"

Then I tell them to begin coughing and to continue coughing until they sense that they are fully free on the inside. (This is the way the Lord has shown me to do it.) Some are delivered with more dramatic experiences than others, but all with the need are delivered. Within about fifteen minutes, most of them come to an inner sensing of great freedom within themselves.

Sometimes, a very small percentage of those present require some personal ministry after the meeting has been dismissed, and two or three times, some have needed more ministry the next day. Most, however, are delivered in this simple way.

These results have been astounding to me. Since 1975, I had been ministering deliverance both to individuals and to groups. I had been taught to name the demons individually and cast them out in the name of Jesus. These ministerings always proved to be lengthy and demanding, taxing to everyone involved.

Identifying demon after demon can be a long process, but casting them out by the anointing is the great blessing every man needs. Many pastors and church leaders and longtime believers have been blessed by submitting to this ministry of deliverance. It is a way to bring the needed benefits of deliverance to the whole body of a church, for the large majority of believers are not aware of their own personal need for deliverance, or are ashamed to come forward to ask for it. And the time this ministry requires is indeed miraculous. I have seen three thousand people delivered in the space of about twenty minutes.

It has been made plain to me that the Body of Christ is very dirty, that demonic captivities are present in many of its members, in some to a greater extent than in others. I believe that the Lord has made known this way of wide and rapid deliverance because we are truly approaching the time of His return, the time when the Body of Christ, His Bride, must be found to be *"without spot or wrinkle."* The need for cleaning is so very great that there is no longer time to spend hours to bring a single person to deliverance. The time is now short, and the Lord requires quick results.

Let me underscore the fact that this ministry of the anointing for deliverance is not something unique to me. I teach everyone (ANYONE) to do the same, and many others are doing it with the same results.

Luke 4:18 deals with burdens and oppressions that the Holy Spirit has been sent to lift from us. As was noted in the previous chapter, Luke 4:19 deals with positive blessings that the Spirit has come to confer upon us: *"The Spirit of the LORD is upon Me, because He has anointed Me... to proclaim the acceptable year of the LORD."* We noted that this refers to the wonderful blessings that God gave to Israel in the year of Jubilee, celebrated each fiftieth year during Old Testament times. Many unique benefits were provided to His people during that year.

Here, in Luke 4, the Lord reveals that this Old Testament practice was but a sign or a shadow of the reality to come when the anointing would come to reside in men. He said that the anointing, recently come upon Him, was to usher in the substance of which the Old Testament Jubilee was but a shadow. It was time for Jesus to proclaim that the true Jubilee had come with the advent of the Holy Spirit, who would reside in men to give blessings through divine power. It was the time when the free favors of God would *"profusely abound,"* as the Amplified Version declares.

Are there positive blessings that you need from God for yourself? For others? For your work in the Kingdom of God? The Spirit says to come to God and take them.

Let us therefore come boldly to the throne of grace, that we may obtain mercy and find grace to help in time of need. Hebrews 4:16, NKJ

Boldly take what you need, for the Father offers it to you graciously. All the blessings we need in life have been provided for us by His love.

So profuse is God's grace toward us now that the blessings we need are already in existence in the spiritual realm. We need but take them by the anointing He has given to us.

> *Blessed be the God and Father of our Lord Jesus Christ [the Anointed One],*
> *who has blessed us with every spiritual blessing in Christ [the Anointed One].*
>
> Ephesians 1:3, NKJ

The blessings we need exist now in the spiritual dimension. God has them waiting for us in the spirit world. He means for them to come to us in the material world. The taking of them is our responsibility, and the process is through Christ, the Anointed One, and that same Holy Spirit anointing Christ has given to us. By the ministry of the anointing, we can receive all that we need in life.

In this verse, the point is that we have all the blessings we need *"in Christ."* These words *"in Christ"* express union with Christ. We have them in union with the anointing on the Lord Jesus, which is now also upon a Spirit-filled believer. Use the anointing to take what God has waiting for you now.

We may minister the anointing for personal blessings that people deeply need and desire. The anointing will flow forth gloriously. The one doing the ministering senses it, and the person receiving senses it. This obviously demonstrates that God is in full accord with what is being done. He is showing that He is now doing that for which the anointing is being ministered.

Can anyone possibly think that the anointing is flowing from the minister only because it is the will of the minister? Can anyone think that God can be forced to manifest Himself or that it is solely the will of a man that is causing the anointing to flow? Can anyone possibly think that God is gloriously manifesting Himself, but is opposed to that for which the anointing is being ministered? This thinking is absurd! The anointing flows because it is God's idea that it flow. The minister is only cooperating with the will of God by taking the steps God has set forth for him to take. God wills to do that for which the Spirit is flowing.

Furthermore, God is not manifesting Himself in the anointing to lead people astray. When the anointing is ministered for healing, and then the manifestation of the anointing appears, God has given that blessing — healing. In His infinite goodness, His great love, His faithfulness to His Word, He could not act differently. The anointing is manifested because the Father wills the blessing sought, and the Holy Spirit is bringing it about.

Here are a few often requested blessings for which I continually minister the anointing to others:

- To obtain a spouse
- For employment
- For mental intelligence and sharpness in exams in school
- To defeat a lawsuit against a believer or against a church
- To have greater insight into the Scriptures
- For financial prosperity

What, if any, are the limits regarding ministering the anointing for blessings needed by a person? I am very limited in my understanding of the infinite goodness and love of God, and of His limitless grace towards men. When I am confronted by doubts as to whether He will give a certain blessing, I turn to the Amplified Version's translation of Luke 4:18-19:

The Spirit of the Lord [is] upon Me, because He has anointed Me [the Anointed One, the Messiah] ... to proclaim the accepted and acceptable year of the Lord [the day when salvation and THE FREE FAVORS OF GOD PROFUSELY ABOUND]. LUKE 4:18-19, AMP

God is not setting limits on the blessings He has available for His people, so why should I? I minister the anointing for the blessing sought and put no limits on God. I cannot forget the pragmatic answer of a blind man healed by the Lord Jesus. He was later criticized by religious Jews, and his answer was: *"All I know is, I was blind and now I see!"*

All I know is this: I minister the anointing for the blessing needed. The anointing is manifested and flows forth to bring the blessing to pass. That's enough for me.

CHAPTER 10

THE MANIFESTATIONS OF THE SPIRIT SPOKEN OF IN FIRST CORINTHIANS 12

Now to each one THE MANIFESTATION OF THE SPIRIT is given for the common good.   1 Corinthians 12:7

The anointing may be ministered to bring forth each of the nine manifestations of the Holy Spirit that are listed in 1 Corinthians 12:8-10.

Verse 11 states that these manifestations are given sovereignly as the Spirit wills. Experience proves that this is so. Often a word of wisdom, a word of prophecy, a discerning of spirits or a healing comes suddenly, unexpectedly, from the Spirit, and the Lord's people are blessed by it.

This verse does not say that these manifestations are limited only to the Spirit's sovereign acts. Actually, the Word of God and experience teach us that it is also the will of the Spirit that these manifestations be brought forth through the initiative and faith of believers. For example, we do not wait for the Spirit to initiate a manifestation of healing. The Word of God teaches us to pray for the sick, and declares that they will be raised up by the prayer of faith.

Paul, in 1 Corinthians 14:31, taught that all may prophesy one by one. When a believer relies in faith on this word, he can prophesy. Also, we are well accustomed to the manifestation of speaking in tongues every time a person begins to speak the words out in faith. I am convinced that it is only because we do not use more faith that our experience has been limited regarding the manifestations listed in 1 Corinthians 12:8-10.

Also, I believe that this view is solidly supported by the Scriptures. In chapter 12 of this passage, we are told that the manifestations of the Spirit come sovereignly as the Spirit wills. In 12:31, we are told that there is a better way that Paul will now show. A better way to what? Paul had been talking about the manifestations of the Spirit that come sovereignly, and he was saying that he was now going to show a better way to have these manifestations than by waiting passively for the Spirit to bring them forth.

In chapter 13, Paul spoke of faith and love. That is the better way, according to the Spirit, of bringing forth God's divine power. Use faith in God and in His Word. Act in love in everything you do to bring on this power. Then, you will see the needed manifestation you hope for.

And now abide faith, hope, love, these three ... .
1 Corinthians 13:13, NKJ

As this verse concludes, the greatest of these three is love, but I believe the Holy Spirit pointed this fact out at this time because of the danger that existed of becoming puffed up in pride as we use our faith and see the wonderful manifestations that result. Love alone will not bring on needed Holy Spirit manifestations. It is faith that brings them on. We are to perform them in love.

More than twenty years ago, the Lord showed me this interpretation, and since then, signs and wonders have abounded in my service to others. I teach the same things to others, and they have the same results. Because of this interpretation and the experience of what it has produced over many years, it was easy for me to accept what the Spirit showed me regarding ministry of the anointing to bring on these manifestations.

Through faith in John 7:37-39, and as one is expressing the desire for the particular manifestation of one of these nine, the Holy Spirit will manifest it.

Ministering the anointing for healing is a common practice in many meetings. Prominent ministers of the anointing continually do this, and marvelous signs and wonders and healings result. I have also found, however, that the anointing may be ministered to oneself and/ or to others regarding all of the other manifestations in the list in 1 Corinthians 12:8-10. A good example of this is prophecy. I have ministered the anointing for the Spirit of prophecy to come upon myself, upon small groups of others or even upon many at the same time.

One morning, I was ministering to a group of about a hundred and twenty people, and I ministered the Spirit of prophecy to the entire group. I had given them scriptural grounds as a basis for their faith, and I had explained their part in the receiving of the anointing. They sought it, and the Holy Spirit responded. It took more than two hours that day as more than a hundred of them came forward and prophesied. It was done one by one in proper scriptural order (see 1 Corinthians 14:31). Everyone can do it, the Scriptures show us, and that day, nearly everyone did.

The ministry of the anointing for prophecy to a believing, willing, open-to-the-Spirit group brings believers to experience this scriptural promise that everyone may prophesy. (In nearly thirty years in Pentecost, I have never seen this happen while people were waiting for the Holy Spirit to move sovereignly.)

Believers who previously have prophesied respond readily when the anointing comes upon them, but we must not limit it to those who have already experienced prophecy. Believers who have never prophesied before must also have an opportunity. After all, we have to start somewhere. Ministering the anointing to those who are new to this experience is a wonderful aid to introduce them to the gift.

People should first be instructed in what will happen to them as the anointing comes upon them. They should be told what is expected of them as the Spirit gives them words or spiritual concepts or visions. They need encouragement to speak forth what has come to them by the Spirit, for they are venturing into new spiritual territory.

The exact same thing is true of a message in tongues and interpretation. The anointing of the Spirit of prophecy will also bring on the interpretation of tongues in the language of those present. It is helpful to gently encourage people who are present to pay attention to the words or thoughts coming to them while the anointing is upon them, so that they can speak them forth.

Some Christians regularly receive a word from the Lord — a word of wisdom or a word of knowledge. Some receive such a word now and then. Most only receive such a word through a sovereign act of God. We may also have such words in time of need at our own initiation. By bringing forth the anointing through faith in the words of John 7:37-39, the Holy Spirit will give us what we need to know. The ministry of the manifestation of the anointing to oneself will do the same.

Regarding miracles, one of my great delights is to demonstrate to believers how God is ever ready to perform them for us. I teach everyone that they may also serve to bring forth a miracle on behalf of another. We know that there are those to whom God has given miracles as a special gift for the Church, and He works miracles regularly through them for the Body. Through these ministries, many miraculous healings come forth.

But, there are other wondrous works that God does that are not readily apparent in our church services. For instance, He sends us extraordinary solutions to complex problems. He causes burdens and or oppressions to be lifted in a short space of time. He miraculously changes financial situations, conditions in nature and difficult circumstances that we may be facing. All these regularly appear in response to the ministry of the anointing for the Spirit of miracles to come upon the one in need of a miracle.

Again, the gift I have is not a gift of working miracles. I have *the gift of God,* the gift of the Holy Spirit, which came upon me when I received the baptism of the Holy Spirit. It is the same extraordinary gift that millions in the Body of Christ have received. What the Lord has shown me regarding the ministry of the anointing for miracles, I do, and I teach others to do the same. The result is miracles.

This ministry is for ANYONE, as the Lord has said. There is no reason whatsoever that there cannot be millions of Christians all over the earth, every day, working miracles. Furthermore, the Lord has told me that before He comes back for His Church, this miraculous type of ac-

113

tivity will indeed be taking place everywhere and many will be involved. This is His desire, and He has enabled us to do it.

This truth is so simple. According to the Word of God, we must do these things:

- Thirst! Ardently desire the needed miracle.
- Come into the presence of the Lord Jesus.
- Drink of Him by our spirits. Drink deeply ... and at length.
- Believe Him.

The Lord has declared that the anointing will flow as we do these things. Believe Him and His Word. Then, declare openly and boldly that the anointing is flowing, and it will flow. It always does.

Chapter 11

The Fruit of the Spirit

But THE FRUIT OF THE SPIRIT is love, joy, peace, patience, kindness, goodness, faithfulness, gentleness and self-control.   Galatians 5:22

Here are presented nine aspects of the character of God, which the Holy Spirit has been sent to manifest in and through men. Although it is the work of the Spirit over a person's entire lifetime to develop and mature these things in him, nevertheless, the Spirit may be ministered at a given time for each one of them.

At the time of such ministry, the anointing of the Spirit will come upon the person who is receiving. He will be filled with the Spirit, who will then manifest that particular fruit within him. Continual ministry of the anointing for each of these fruits will help greatly in Christ-like behavioral development.

When a person is confronted with a need, or a desire, for one of these gifts at a particular time or for a particular purpose, the anointing may be ministered. That fruit will then be forthcoming in the matter at hand, sometimes in a dramatic way.

The Spirit of God is all of the following:

- The Spirit of Love
- The Spirit of Joy
- The Spirit of Peace
- The Spirit of Patience
- The Spirit of Kindness
- The Spirit of Goodness

- The Spirit of Faithfulness
- The Spirit of Gentleness
- The Spirit of Self-control

Anyone may minister the anointing according to the steps the Lord gives in John 7:37-39, so that the Spirit manifests Himself in each of these aspects of holiness. The anointing may be ministered to oneself, to another or to many others — even to a person or persons who are not present. The anointing flows.

The fruits of the Spirit are expressions of the nature of God, of the nature of the Spirit of God. A human being is created to reflect the image and likeness of God. The Spirit has come to men to express these things through them, the Spirit being the origin and source of these fruits. Furthermore, the Spirit has come to dwell within a man in order to express His godly nature through that man in these behavioral expressions.

In view of these considerations, it becomes understandable how readily the anointing flows when ministered for one of these fruits of the Spirit. Oh, how God desires these fruits to be the normal behavior of His people! No wonder that a considerable number of the more dramatic and impacting manifestations of the anointing that I have seen have occurred when the anointing has been ministered for the fruit of the Spirit.

JOY

In 1994, it was this delightful expression of God's Spirit in a human that served to introduce me into conscious and purposeful ministry of the anointing. Like most believers, I had had frequent experience with the anointing manifested to me — in intimate prayer, in anointed worship services, in special times of revelation, in teaching and in preaching the Word of God. But in March of 1994, Brother Rodney Howard-Browne was conducting a three-week seminar in a church in Maryland. There were reports of uncontrollable laughter and other unique expressions of joy being manifested in the meetings. I questioned whether such behavior was of the Spirit of God. Never having

The Fruit of the Spirit

seen such things in the fifty years I had been involved in the things of the Lord, I attributed it to some sort of emotionalism. Therefore, I had no interest in attending his meetings.

How prejudiced we are and how quickly we jump out for or against a matter! In this case, as is often true, this was a serious matter. What was taking place was coming from an infinite God, but I was rejecting it out of hand because I was judging by my own experience, my own understanding and my own traditions. This did not line up with what I had been taught. (A noted writer once said, "I never allow my education to get in the way of my learning.") Fortunately for me, a friend of mine had a mind and heart open to the Spirit and he insisted that I accompany him to one of those meetings. I reluctantly agreed.

In the meetings, I saw people laughing with great joy. Many fell to the floor, often rolling over and over while laughing uproariously. Some of them were exhibiting behavior I had never before seen in a church service. And this was not a momentary reaction. These things went on for hours.

I was ill at ease, critical of such behavior, uncomfortable at seeing it tolerated in church and perplexed, but at the same time I was filled with wonder at all of these strange happenings. It seemed undeniable to me that the anointing of the Holy Spirit was strongly upon the meeting. God didn't seem to mind the apparent disorder at all. As the meeting went on for about five hours, it gradually dawned on me that it was God who was causing what I had labeled "disorder."

After that, you couldn't keep me away from the meetings. Of the thirty-six sessions in the seminar, I attended thirty-three. I was drawn, most of all, by the joy being expressed by the people. I could see that it was truly the joy of the Lord.

The Holy Spirit was expressing His joy through people, in a dimension beyond the joy I had always known as a Christian in union with the Spirit. Through human temples, the Spirit was manifesting some part of the infinite joy that was part of His infinite being. And the joy He was expressing was clearly not natural to a human. I was to learn that this brought great delight to God to so bless His beloved children. I know it was a joy to watch.

The Bible speaks of "joy unspeakable and full of glory," and that is what the manifestation of the anointing was causing to come forth from God's people. What a mind expander this was for me! I experienced a sudden amplification of my understanding of what God is like. His joy is beyond the limits of my understanding and experience. Of course, He would express a portion of this great joy through men. How could He not? Did He not make us to reflect His image and His likeness? It was all so new to me, but it was also very clear.

As I continued to attend the seminar, the Lord began telling me to bring these teachings on the anointing to my friends in churches in Colombia, South America. In 1972, I had been living in Cali, Colombia, when the Lord filled me with the Spirit during a great Charismatic revival that took place there. Then, in 1980, I had returned to the United States to work in some matters the Lord had called me to. Now, the Lord was telling me that it was time to go back. He wanted the anointing and manifestation of His joy to be known among His Colombian people.

Suddenly, I found myself with a great problem. I was willing to go, and I knew the people the Lord wanted me to minister to. But how was I to minister this joy? Exactly what did I need to do so that the anointing would come forth with this manifestation?

I began analyzing the way that Brother Rodney was ministering. He began during the time of worship to lead the people in choruses of worship and adoration and love. As He continued, the anointing of the Spirit became stronger and stronger, sweeter and sweeter. The anointing was coming forth on the voice of the singer.

Brother Rodney has a rich baritone voice, and it pulled me into worship as he ministered in song. Gradually, people in the congregation began to laugh. The laughter became greater and more widespread. Frequently, it became uncontrollable by those who were blessed by it.

As I watched this same pattern each day, I puzzled before the Lord at what He was telling me to do: "Bring the anointing for joy and laughter to your friends in Colombia." The plain truth was that I had never been able to carry a tune and I was terrible at singing any type of song or hymn. In times of worshiping the Lord, my natural singing voice had always resulted in "fracturing" the anointing for the people around me. Now I thought, *Me? Lead people in worship for the anointing to fall on them? Lord, You've got to be kidding!*

Nevertheless, I knew that the Lord was indeed telling me to go to Colombia regarding ministering the anointing. I set myself to study the Word of God and to prepare the messages I would be giving when I arrived in Colombia. I had been used by the Lord to teach the Bible, but very seldom to preach. My service to others had been in the analysis of the Word, giving explanations and insights regarding the Scriptures. Now, I studied what the Word had to say about the anointing, and examined how the anointing was ministered in the Bible.

Then one day, as I was studying, the words of John 7:37-39 struck me. This was my answer. By following the pattern laid out by Jesus in these verses, I could minister the anointing so that the Spirit of joy would come upon the people — without having to sing and lead others in worship. I came to realize that the Lord was showing me that the anointing could be ministered to bring about a particular aspect of the Holy Spirit — in this case, joy.

As I meditated upon these verses, the Holy Spirit opened them further to me. I saw that the Lord was indeed teaching that by faith in this Word and in Him ANYONE could minister the anointing of the Holy Spirit. If one thirsted for it, or desired a particular manifestation — in this case, joy — that would be what the Spirit brought forth. I would not have to sing after all. I was thrilled.

The experience of walking out the things I had learned was wonderful, and as I began to conduct seminars on what I had learned, my understanding increased. As always, the Lord showed Himself faithful to His Word.

As the months went by and my "holy investigations" continued, I learned that the same was true for many other manifestations of the Spirit. I learned that anyone can minister the anointing anywhere, not only in believer's meetings. Music, singing, the creation of a religious atmosphere ... none of these were essential for the Spirit to flow. The Lord set forth certain things to do. If I would do them, the anointing would flow. And this would work for ANYONE willing to lend heart faith to the Lord and His Word. Today, many thousands have learned to do the same.

There are several important things I must say about the joy of the Lord that the anointing often brings forth from a person:

1. *"The joy of the Lord is your strength"* (Nehemiah 8:10). This over-flowing with joy that the anointing brings will produce:

   • Strength during trials and difficulties.
   • Strength that results in a release of inner tensions.
   • Cleansing from inner burdens. Then the Holy Spirit is able to flow out from one more easily.
   • Strength that helps to break down religiosity and legalistic ritualism.

   I have seen many examples in which the anointing for this supernatural joy came upon people who had been undergoing great trials or hardships. As they continued under that anointing for days, the trials disappeared miraculously. Also, during the time people are engulfed with great laughter and joy while under this anointing, many are delivered from the influence of demonic spirits.

2. There are people who criticize this uncontrollable laughter in others while they are under the anointing of the Spirit of joy. Some say this is simply a lack of order in the meeting. First, we must say that the Holy Spirit is Lord — Lord of all, and He can do what He wishes. He is Lord over any meeting being held to honor God. Men ought to learn to accommodate themselves to His idea of what order is and not hold fast to their own ideas on the subject. In this great move of the Spirit that we are witnessing in the world today, the anointing is doing things that are new to all of us. Our traditions, our past experiences, our reasoned theological positions, our denominational customs, our non-familiarity with the ways of the Spirit ... all these are great enemies of the freedom the Spirit requires that He may operate freely in our midst. By all means, let us test the Spirit, but not by the flesh, nor by reason. Let us examine the fruits of what is

happening. Let us be sensitive to the Spirit of God in these new things. Let us be led by the Spirit in the meetings wherever He will take us. Let us not constrict nor restrict moves of the Spirit by our puny human understanding.

Please! Let us not find ourselves in the position of trying to limit God in what He can do among us. What a strange thing! People going to church to honor God and then rejecting Him and His deeds when He shows up personally to bless them!

3. Regarding the uncontrollable joy of the Lord that the Spirit brings to one, the anointing did this very thing to the Lord Jesus:

> *And the seventy returned again with joy, saying, Lord, even the devils are subject unto us through thy name.*
> *And he said unto them, I beheld Satan as lightning fall from heaven. Behold, I give you power to tread on serpents and scorpions, and over all the power of the enemy; and nothing shall by any means hurt you. Notwithstanding, in this rejoice not, that the spirits are subject unto you; but rather rejoice, because your names are written in heaven.*
> *In that hour Jesus rejoiced in spirit ... .*   Luke 10:17-21, KJV
> (The NIV says, *"Jesus, full of joy through the Holy Spirit... ."*)

This word *"joy"* in verse 17 and this word *"rejoice"* in verse 20 are translated from the Greek word meaning "cheerfulness, calm delight, be happy, be glad." In verse 21, however, the word *"rejoice"* used to describe the behavior of the Lord Jesus is from a different word, one that the Greeks used to describe a kind of joy that one expressed. It means that Jesus jumped for joy. He exulted. He became exceedingly glad. He rejoiced greatly. He rejoiced with exceeding joy.

These all describe what the Spirit of joy is bringing to believers in anointed meetings all over the world today. Those who have experienced this anointing for joy understand well what the Lord Himself experienced here — explosive and uncontrollable joy in the Spirit.

What a great difficulty it would present to many religious, straitlaced people today if they saw the Lord Jesus act this way! This is the same difficulty they have with the joy so many thousands of open-hearted believers are experiencing under the anointing of the precious Spirit of joy.

LOVE

Galatians 5:22 shows us that the fruit of the Spirit is love, God's love. There is so much to deal with regarding God's love — His love for all mankind and His love for each and every individual. He desires that His love be expressed through us toward others, and when it is, the effect is awesome. What rich matters for study and meditation! But here we must limit our focus to the Spirit of love and the ministry of the anointing to manifest divine love to and then through any individual or group.

Second Timothy 1:7 shows us that we have been given the spirit of love, and the Holy Spirit has been revealed to us as being the Spirit of Love Himself. Romans 5:5 tells us: *"The love of God is shed abroad in our hearts by the Holy Ghost [Spirit] which is given to us"* (KJV). This is the Spirit that dwells in us, and this is the kind of divine Love that God wills to be manifested to men and through men.

We were created to show forth the image and likeness of our Creator. He, by the Spirit of love He has put in us, wills that love to be manifested to us and through us to others. God wants every man and woman to know, personally and experientially, the love He has for him or her. It is only by the Spirit of love that this can be accomplished.

Romans 5:5 speaks of the love of God *"shed abroad [or poured out] in our hearts."* God is not trying to keep His love a secret from men, and neither does He expect us to receive by faith alone the fact that He loves us. It is true that the Word of God tells us of His love for us, but He also desires to lavishly pour out that love in a deep and full manifestation.

This is exactly what happens when the anointing for the Spirit of love is ministered according to John 7:37-39. The Holy Spirit comes upon the one receiving. That person becomes filled to overflowing, as the love of God bathes his inner being. He becomes filled with the delights of the divine love of God.

The Fruit of the Spirit

This ministry of the anointing needs to be experienced. It cannot be explained otherwise. I, for one, cannot fully express in words the things God has shown me, and I have seen only the beginnings. God has for us what Paul described as *"the breadth, and length, and depth, and height"* of *"the love of Christ"* (Ephesians 3:18-19, KJV). The Spirit desires us *"to know the love of Christ, which passeth knowledge, that [we] might be filled with all the fulness of God"* (Verse 19, KJV).

The Spirit of love may be ministered to flow between spouses, and it should be done often. The love a man and a woman share will thus deepen, and love will be expressed by them for each other as never before. I have seen married couples who were locked in strife with one another come to genuine peace with each other, through the ministry of the Spirit of love, each to the other.

The Spirit of love may be ministered by parents to their children and by children to their parents, and it should be done often. A deepening and widening of their love will be the result.

The Spirit of love may be ministered between believers, and it should be done often. The Spirit of love may be ministered to persons who are not present at the time of the ministry. The anointing will flow forth and deal with those persons.

I delight, daily, in ministering the Spirit of love to myself. I want to experience God's love continually and to grow in the knowledge of His love. Experiencing His love causes my love toward Him to increase (see 1 John 4:12).

MINISTERING THE SPIRIT OF LOVE

To minister the anointing for the Spirit of love, one needs simply to get heart-involved with the four things the Lord teaches in John 7:37-39:

1. Lord, I desire deeply that the Spirit of love come upon this person.
2. Lord, I come into Your presence.
3. Lord I drink of You. My spirit draws You to myself.
4. Lord, I believe, at my words of faith, that the Spirit of love now comes upon this person.

"In the name of the Lord Jesus, the Spirit of love comes upon you now."

Wait in the presence of the Lord, continually drinking of Him, and the anointing will flow to fill the person receiving.

MINISTERING THE SPIRIT OF PEACE

The lack of peace is something most of us experience every day in the many and different circumstances we encounter and in the many different people with whom we come in contact. We are confronted on all sides with anxiety, stress, worry and inner upheavals of all sorts. Still, the anointing that is within us is the Spirit of Peace. We can receive this blessing whenever we need it. We ought to learn to be generous in ministering it to others. Ministering the Spirit of peace to others is a wonderful way to introduce them to the person of the Lord Jesus, for the person of the Lord is Himself our peace. This ministry is a precious tool for evangelization.

The anointing may be ministered in this same way for the six fruits we did not cover. As each of these fruits is needed, the anointing will flow.

CHAPTER 12

TO CONFIRM A WORD OF GOD

Nevertheless I tell you the truth; It is expedient for you that I go away: for if I go not away, the Comforter will not come unto you; but if I depart, I will send him unto you.   John 16:7, KJV

So then, after the Lord had spoken unto them, he was received up into heaven, and sat on the right hand of God. And they went forth, and preached every where, the Lord working with them, and confirming the word with signs following. Amen.   Mark 16:19-20, KJV

The Lord Jesus sent the Spirit to do things for us. In John 16:7, the Lord explained to His disciples that in His going away they would greatly benefit. It was the plan of God that, from Heaven, the Lord Jesus would send the Holy Spirit to dwell with them and to work with them. The Spirit would then be at work in the earth wherever believers were found. The work of the Spirit would no longer be limited to a place where the Lord Jesus was present physically, as had been the case during His time on earth.

In Mark 16:19-20, there is set forth a fulfilling, in part, of what the Lord meant by the great benefit to the disciples of the Spirit being with them. He would do for them and through their ministry the works of the Lord Jesus, and *"even greater things"* than He did (John 14:12).

In Mark 16:20, there is a revelation that opens up many areas to the ministry of the anointing. It says that the Lord confirmed His Word by the signs that accompanied it. The Lord confirms His Word. He backs up what His Word says by giving Holy Spirit manifestations in accord

125

with what a particular scripture has declared. He does what the Word says, and this is confirmation that the word is true.

Since I believe the promise of Mark 16:20, that the Spirit is with us to confirm His Word, I act according to my faith. I take a specific word of God, and I minister the anointing to confirm that word in the meeting where I am teaching. When I do this, the Spirit does in the congregation exactly what that word said He would do. Obviously, this opens the door for ministry of the anointing into fields beyond measure.

In meetings, in order to demonstrate how ANYONE can minister the power of the anointing according to faith in John 7:37-39, I often present a given verse to the congregation. I lead them to receive what it says into their hearts. I then minister the anointing to confirm that word. The Holy Spirit always flows forth upon everyone present and He does in them exactly what that word said He would do. Thus, He confirms His Word by signs following.

SOME EXAMPLES

1. *"You anoint my head with oil; my cup runs over"* (Psalm 23:5, NKJ). I announce and explain this word, and then I minister the anointing. The Holy Spirit comes upon everyone, and each one begins to fill up. Some receive visions, or revelations, or other personally needed blessings, but they all receive in overflowing measure.

   It is simple. I proclaim the word to the people, and then I minister the anointing to confirm what it says. As everyone waits on the Lord, in His presence, with everyone drinking of Him, the anointing begins to flow. It flows and flows and flows some more ... until the people become filled to overflowing.

2. *"I will not leave you orphans. I will come to you"* (John 14:18, NKJ). Ministering the anointing to confirm this verse brings upon everyone present the manifested presence of the Lord Jesus and with it, His great comforts, His sweetness and His personal delights. This ministry has profound effects upon many, for there are people who truly are orphans and have been so since childhood.

There are other people who are hurting greatly within themselves from loneliness and or lack of affection from others toward them. There are others who have been rejected or who have been battered by the circumstances of life. There are many who do not know the comfort of protecting, caring, loving parents. There are many who are just plain empty within. Some have covered themselves over with a veneer that hides from view these and other such hurts and lacks.

As the anointing comes upon the people to confirm this verse, the Holy Spirit reveals the Lord Jesus to them. They experience His consoling, comforting workings. The concrete walls that encircle them within begin to crack and to break up. They sense deep release, as inner healing is ministered to them by the Spirit. They experience what they deeply need ... the knowledge that they are not alone. The Lord Jesus is with them. He cares for them, and He is showing them that He cares.

Many react with deep sobbing and with tears. These are not tears of sadness, but tears of washing and of cleansing. This goes on at length, finally effecting a most wonderful inner comfort and assurance. The Holy Spirit has confirmed His word with signs and wonders. He has done this very word in those who heard it preached.

3. *"He [the Holy Spirit] will convict the world of sin"* (John 16:8, NKJ). I have proclaimed this word to large groups, and then I have ministered the anointing to the people to confirm its promise. As a result, people have come forward to repent and to receive salvation. They testified of the strong conviction of sin that had come over them.

    Also, believers in such a meeting come under conviction for sins they have been tolerating in their lives for some time. They testify, at times, of dramatic means of conviction of sin that they experienced while under this anointing. Some even have visions of the Lord Jesus, and through them He convicts them personally.

4. *"The love of God is shed abroad in our hearts by the Holy Ghost [Spirit] which is given unto us"* (Romans 5:5, KJV). As the people open up their hearts to receive this word and to receive the anointing, the Spirit of love comes upon them in great sweetness and depth. Some are literally transported into raptures of divine love.

There are other verses that I have sometimes used to demonstrate that the anointing will confirm a particular word of God right then and right there in a meeting. But, because of the nature of my ministry, I find myself often repeating the same teachings again and again, and I often use the same verses to give demonstrations. How wonderful it would be to stay with one group for an extended time, for I sense that the Lord desires to demonstrate His power on our behalf in many new areas that I have not yet experienced.

There is so much new ground to explore in the Scriptures regarding ministering the anointing to confirm the Word of God. This is a place for holy boldness. This is a place to learn what new things the anointing wills to do before the Lord Jesus returns.

THE SPIRIT OF ...

The anointing is the Spirit of Wisdom, the Spirit of Healing, the Spirit of Deliverance, the Spirit of Holiness, the Spirit of Peace, the Spirit of Prophecy, the Spirit of Life in Christ Jesus, the Spirit of Prosperity, the Spirit of Truth, the Spirit of Promise, etc. He will confirm His word on each of these points that reveal what and who He is. He will behave as each verse declares Him to be.

Throughout the Scriptures, much is revealed about the nature of the Spirit of God. In the use of this expression, "the Spirit of _____," we are given insight into what He is like in Himself. Each time used, this expresses how He is (His nature), and how He behaves, or desires to behave, in the earth.

The Lord Jesus sent the Spirit of God to men to behave among us as God wants to behave among us. The Lord said that the Spirit would *"guide [us] into all truth"* (John 16:13). This includes truth about God, and how He wills to act in creation. This expression tells us what He is like and what He will do, how He wants to reveal Himself in His creation.

In *Strong's Concordance*, I count more than one hundred and fifty expressions of who the Spirit is, with different adjectives describing what He is or does. Each of these tells us something basic about the Spirit of God. I have ministered the anointing through some thirty-five to forty expressions of the Spirit. Always, the anointing has flowed forth from me to do that which He is the Spirit of. I am continuing to learn in this area, as new opportunities and new situations arise. I want to learn more and see more of what God is like.

In any given situation, where there is a present need of supply of that which the Spirit is, the anointing flows forth to give the needed provision. When we walk out John 7:37-39, the Spirit acts accordingly.

I look ahead with anticipation. The future will most certainly present opportunities and needs for the anointing to reveal new signs and wonders concerning what God is like. Consider these possibilities:

- He is the Spirit *"for the display of his splendor"* (Isaiah 61:3).
- He is *"the Spirit of glory"* (1 Peter 4:14).
- He is *"the Spirit of power"* (Isaiah 11:2). (Remember how the Spirit acted through Samson.)
- He is *"the Spirit"* of *"unity"* (Ephesians 4:3).

CHAPTER 13

MINISTERING THE ANOINTING TO ONESELF FOR PERSONAL PROVISION

"Everyone who drinks this water will be thirsty again, but whoever drinks the water I give him will never thirst. Indeed, the water I give him will become in him a spring of water welling up to eternal life."
John 4:13-14

There are more teachings of the Lord Jesus on the Holy Spirit and ministry of the anointing in the gospel of John than in the other three gospels. In chapters 3 and 4 of John's gospel, we are introduced to the Lord's teaching on the Spirit. In these portions, He teaches on the role of the Spirit in the believer in whom He has come to dwell.

In chapter 3, He tells Nicodemus of the necessity of the new birth, His metaphor for what happens to a believer through the activity of the Holy Spirit, when He comes to reside in him. The Holy Spirit comes to a believer to do specific things in and through the life of that person. There is then present a new life to give that person a whole new way of living. That new life is the life of God by the Holy Spirit. The Holy Spirit has come to that person for his personal supply and provision, and for expression through him. This will all take place by the activity of the divine life present in him.

Then, in chapter 4, the Lord goes further regarding the Holy Spirit's supply for life for that person. In verses 10 and 14, He teaches the Samaritan woman that the Holy Spirit comes to a person for that person's supply and provision in every aspect of his life. The Holy

Ministering the Anointing to Oneself for Personal Provision

Spirit anointing comes to a believer to do things which can only be done by the life of God. The Spirit is within him to "well up" for eternal life, says the Lord Jesus. That is, the Spirit is to come forth with His blessings from that person. The Spirit of God is to be within the believer as the continuing source for participation in the very life of God.

Most of us have focused our activity in the anointing on ministry to others for their needed supply, for example, their healing, their filling with the Spirit, etc. Certainly this is valid ministry. It is desirable and very necessary. But, at the same time, too many of us have overlooked the ministry of the anointing to ourselves. Jesus dealt with this need in His teachings here in chapter 4 of John.

The ministry of the anointing, or, as some term it, the transfer of the anointing or the impartation of the anointing to other people, is often a dramatic occurrence. From one individual in whom the anointing dwells, that same Almighty, divine Spirit of God flows forth in power to have an impact upon, and to work wonders in, another human being. How awesome! How overwhelming!

Now, these acts have become more widespread than ever before.

But let each believer who has the indwelling Holy Spirit also understand the great need of ministering the anointing to himself. These teachings in John 4 are important to us. We must have our own needs met.

The truth is that the Holy Spirit has come to us, first of all, for our requirements. Our supply to others, though important, must be secondary. In this chapter, let us analyze the great wisdom and treasure that is contained in our vessels. We have the anointing within.

John related the fact that Jesus decided to take a trip to Galilee. He had been in Judea, in the neighborhood of Jerusalem, to the south of Galilee. To get back to Galilee, He had to go north, and on the way, He had to pass through Samaria.

John says that Jesus came first to a town in Samaria called Sychar, which appears on a map to be about forty-five kilometers from Jerusalem. He arrived at Sychar at the sixth hour, or twelve noon, in the heat of the day.

The Lord made this journey on foot, walking this distance, and it took Him until noon to reach His destination. This long walk, over mountainous terrain and desert lands, apparently took Jesus seven or eight hours. To get there at noon, therefore, He would have had to get up at about 3 A.M., make preparations and set out on the trip.

After His long trek, Jesus immediately headed to the town well for a drink. He was exhausted. He was too tired even to accompany the disciples, who went on into the town to obtain food. He stayed alone at the well, overcome with great thirst.

Jesus sat down near the well, waiting for someone to come along with a means of drawing the water His body craved. What a perfect parallel is presented here with the need of human beings for the life of God to give them their necessary provisions. Every man needs water. Every man needs the indwelling anointing.

Jesus took advantage of His own need for material water to explain to a Samaritan woman who came by about man's need for the indwelling Spirit, and what He told her speaks to us as well. "Look!" the Word of God is telling us. "Look at the vital need the human body of Jesus had for natural water."

Every part of Jesus' body needed water in order to stay alive and continue to function properly. This is basic to every human body. When a body is physically active, as was the body of the Lord on His arduous trip, it uses up its supply of water and needs to replenish that supply. In these moments, the mouth and tongue sense thirst, but they are merely the agents of all the other members and organs of the body. Every part of the body needs water to function. The activities of the body always result in the need for replenishment of water for all of its parts.

This is a continual, everyday matter. A body must have water intake regularly. It must take water into itself in order to function well. The Lord spoke of this need to the Samaritan woman when she came to the well to fill her waterpot.

The woman showed surprise that a Jew would speak to her, for the Jews and the Samaritans were enemies. They had no dealings with each other. This breach was caused by their very different views on religion. Their religious practices were very different, and this had caused bitterness to develop between them.

Jesus ignored these differences and went right to the lesson the Holy

Spirit wanted to give here. He spoke to the woman of the gift of God to man, the Holy Spirit, which Jesus likened to natural water. The gift of God, the Holy Spirit, who will be in a person, comes to him in order to supply provision for his life in all of its aspects, in the same way that natural water is the vital supply to the human body for the healthy functioning of all of its parts.

The Lord Jesus says that this gift of God will be as living water, that is, a kind of water that has life in itself. Natural water promotes life. It fosters and nourishes life, but it does not have life in itself. This living water is so much more. It will cause the life of a person to flourish — whatever it touches and wherever it touches it.

This is the point that the Lord is making. There is as much need, and more, for this living water, the life of God, for the proper, healthy functioning of a human being, than there is need for natural water for his body.

The Lord goes on, in verses 13 and 14:

"Everyone who drinks this water will be thirsty again, but whoever drinks the water I give him will never thirst. Indeed, the water I give him will become in him a spring of water welling up to eternal life." John 4:13-14

Once this living water comes into a person, Jesus shows, it is in him to stay. It will be with him his entire lifetime. It will be in him the source of supply for his needs throughout life. That person will never go thirsty, for his source of supply is always within him.

Jesus said that this living water in us would be like *"a spring of water,"* or, as the King James Version says, *"a well of water,"* a continuous source of provision for the individual. The eternal life of God will be within him always, ever ready to give supply for his needs. All aspects of His life will always be at hand — whatever is needed, at all times — for his physical life, for his financial life, for his marital life, for his career, for his family life, for his spiritual life and for his ministry life.

The Lord says that the living water, the anointing of the Spirit, will be in a believer as a well, even as the natural water near Him was in a well. The water of a well does not gush forth. In this natural example of Jesus near the well in Sychar, He needed water that was deep down in the well, and He had no means of reaching it to draw it up. The water was there, but until someone came along to draw it up in a bucket, it was of no use to Him. This, then, was His focus: a well containing water that needs to be drawn out in order to be of use to someone.

Jesus was not thinking of the *"rivers of living water"* of which John 7:37-39 speaks. In that passage, rivers of water are flowing out from a believer for the benefit of others. Those benefiting will simply receive the waters that flow out and wash over them. They are not actively causing the waters to come to them.

At times, those *"rivers of living water"* flow over thousands at a given time. They bathe everyone abundantly. They bring about various signs and wonders in gathered multitudes. There are rivers flowing. But in John 4:14, Jesus is talking not of rivers for others coming forth, but of a well placed in each believer, from which water must be drawn. As a believer needs supply, water must be drawn out to meet his needs. Then, when a new need presents itself, more supply must again be drawn out, and so on.

Supply will always be present. The well will never go dry. But the water will have to be drawn out, and it must be drawn by the person himself in whom the well has been placed.

The Lord is referring to the Holy Spirit anointing present in a believer. The Spirit is present in the believer, an inexhaustible depository, as it were, of living waters. And, as with a material well, the supply of the blessing must be drawn forth. It will not flow forth as does a river, which does not need help from the one receiving its blessings to make it flow.

The Lord would say to us today, "Look at Me! My Body needs water as I go about My daily living. I must seek out supply from wells. It must be drawn out for Me to benefit from it. Each of you needs living water in every activity of your living. You have been given all the supply for it that you will ever need. It is within you in the person of the Holy Spirit. But it will not come forth to bless you unless it is drawn forth. YOU must bring it forth. YOU must learn to draw forth your needed provision yourself."

So great is the need for a human to have living water for every aspect of his life that the source of its supply will be within the person himself; instant availability present for every needed supply. We are being taught here that man has been created as a dependent being, dependent on the Spirit of God to furnish divine life for all that a man is and does. He is so utterly dependent on the life of God for healthy living and right functioning that his Creator has fashioned him as a container. As a container, he is perfectly formed so as to contain that divine life within himself. This is so, that man may continually draw upon God for supply as he goes about his daily living.

The Lord teaches this same basic principle for healthy and prosperous functioning in John 15, in the parable of the true vine and the branch. He directs each believer to abide in Him, even as a branch abides in a vine. A branch that is attached to a vine is in intimate proximity with that vine, and it continually receives the life of the vine for its healthy living and prosperous activity. The branch is an active partaker of the sap of the vine.

As has been noted, a bucket is needed to draw water from a well. I find that the "bucket" to draw water from the well that is the Spirit within us is revealed in John 7:37-39. The same instructions given by the Lord on how to minister the anointing to others will also cause the anointing to well up within us to give us personal supply. Whether it is to cause rivers of the anointing to flow out to others or to draw the anointing within for ourselves, we must each go through the same steps:

If anyone IS THIRSTY,
let him COME TO ME
and DRINK.
Whoever BELIEVES in me ...

The anointing will flow from a believer in whom the Spirit dwells, to do all the things that the Spirit has been sent by the Lord Jesus to do in and for mankind. But the anointing will also flow from within a believer, in whom the Spirit dwells, on his own behalf.

One may minister the anointing to oneself, to all aspects of one's life, for all things that pertain to his life and to godliness. One need never thirst, and thirst in vain, for needed provision, for the well of supply is within us. Draw it forth continually. Do we not take water or other liquids to ourselves ten to fifteen times each day? Do likewise with the living waters from the well within you — for any and every need.

SOME EXAMPLES

1. Holiness: The anointing is the Spirit of Holiness. The name most frequently given to the anointing within us is that of the HOLY Spirit. He is Holy, separate from all things alien and foreign to God. He is totally separate unto the things of God. He possesses godly behavior, godly living, godly deeds, godly plans and godly purposes.
   I minister the anointing for holiness to myself every day, and I do it more than once a day. I need manifested in me and through me the holiness that our Lord is and that I am not without Him.
   This is especially true regarding sin. The more I have to do with ministry of the anointing to others, the more I see growing in me the desire to live without sin in my life.

2. Prosperity: I minister the Spirit of prosperity to myself daily — without fail. I know what it is to be in poverty, and I know what it is to be in plenty. What a wonderful revelation it was to me that God's will for me and for all of His children is prosperity. I manage my finances according to the principles of giving in the Word of God, and I draw from the well within me the anointing for personal prosperity. Financial blessings continue to come to me.

3. Work: I minister the anointing daily in the matters of my work, both regarding the service the Lord has given me to do and the natural things that confront me. In this present life, burdens and oppressions present themselves from many different sources. But the anointing has been given to me to lift those burdens and to destroy those yokes. It has been given to me to enable me to do all my work well. I draw from the well within me the ample supply for all provision needed.

4. Our Treasure within: In the verses included in 2 Corinthians 2:12-4:6, Paul teaches much on the indwelling Holy Spirit. Then in 4:7, he proclaims that we have this Treasure in the earthen vessels that we are. The Holy Spirit within a human being is there as a treasure for us.

    Anyone who has a treasure has the wherewithal to obtain all the supply needed in his life. A person who has treasure and who lives in lack of supply, lives so either out of ignorance of the treasure's existence, out of laziness in its use or in plain stupidity.

    A believer with the baptism of the Holy Spirit has within him the divine Treasure that the Spirit is. This Treasure is for his personal use, for his own supply — to lift burdens, to destroy oppressions, to give all provision needed for life and for godliness.

    By ministering the anointing to himself for things needed, a person can draw from the inexhaustible Treasure, the unlimited power to supply that this Treasure has. It is plain stupidity to be rich with this Treasure and yet remain living in want or under burdens or oppressions.

5. Physical needs: I minister the anointing to myself for the needs of my body. I need healing at times. I want to maintain my health. I want strength in my seventy-two-year-old bones. I take to myself the anointing against sickness or any weakness. The anointing within me gives the supply needed.

6. The Spirit of Love: I minister the Spirit of love to myself daily. The love of God continues doing its work in me, increasing my love toward God, increasing my love toward others and increasing my obedience to God's Word.

HOW TO MINISTER THE ANOINTING TO YOURSELF

To bring others into a personal awareness of this great Treasure that is in them, I first see to it that each has the baptism of the Holy Spirit.

Then, I tell each person to identify a personal and present need for provision that he or she has. Then, we proceed to a demonstration that the anointing will flow from within each as the Spirit begins to bring that provision to them.

I tell each to place his or her hands upon the belly (for the well is in their innermost parts). I lead them, slowly, into heart involvement with the four steps of John 7:37-39:

1. Lord, how deeply I thirst for (this provision)! How I need this, Lord Jesus! How much I desire and want this!
2. For this need, I seek Your presence, Lord. I seek You, Lord. You are the divine life of God. You are my all in all, all my supply in this my need. I need You and Your presence, Lord.
3. And now I drink of You, my Lord. My spirit draws You to me.
4. I believe, Lord, that You will have the anointing well up within me to give me this provision.

Then, we all speak out our faith, boldly:

"In Your name, Lord Jesus, the anointing now flows within me for this matter."

We wait in the presence of the Lord, and we continue drinking of Him. The anointing now comes up within each, manifesting that the Spirit is, indeed, now at work to bring forth the provision for which each is thirsting.

In this demonstration, the anointing is manifested in all, but it is not ministered by me. Each one has been ministering the anointing to himself. Each one needs to know, through personal experience, that he can minister the anointing to himself.

The rising of the anointing in each person is God showing each one: "Yes! I am now moving in this." The anointing, Himself, is the assurance of this. For, the anointing does not manifest Himself except that the matter in question is, indeed, according to the will of God. God does not fool people. The manifested anointing is proof positive that He is in full accord with the ministry for the desired provision.

Ministering the Anointing to Oneself for Personal Provision

REALITY

Let us remember some basic matters. In Old Testament times, the anointing resided permanently in no one after Adam. But this is not the case today. The cry of David, in Psalm 51:11 (NKJ), *"Do not take Your Holy Spirit from me!"* is not a cry for a New Testament saint. David was anointed to rule as king. The Spirit came upon him for his work as ruler, but after the work was over, the manifested anointing left him. David loved it when the anointing was upon him, but the Spirit did not dwell within him permanently. How that man would have loved to have the anointing with him twenty-four hours a day.

Today, the anointing, the Holy Spirit, is permanently present in believers (see 1 John 2:20 and 27). Whether or not I am sensing the anointing at a given moment, the anointing is always with me. The well is present in me. The anointing does not come to me and depart from me. The manifestation of the anointing may be present, or it may not be present, but the well is always present within me.

The well is ever ready to give me a supply of living water for my needed provisions. By using my faith in the words of John 7:37-39, I may draw forth the manifested anointing from the well. Furthermore, it is the earnest desire of the Lord that I do so continually in my life.

Having placed the well within us, it is God's plan that we live by drawing living water from within ourselves. He does not want us to live only by the flow of the anointing coming from other believers.

I was born into God's Kingdom as a child spiritually, but the expectation is that I grow to be a spiritual adult. The Father does not want me ever living as a child (see 1 John 2:12-14). A child is one who lives by receiving its needs from adults. Adults live according to provisions they make for themselves.

In spiritual adulthood, there is to be a continual drawing of the life of God from the well within each believer. A baby lives only by what others have to give it. It needs to draw its life from the milk of its mother's breast. It is helpless and ignorant to do anything else. But as that baby gets on in years, this ought to change. At age twenty-one, if it is still seeking its mother's breast for its life's needs, something is terribly wrong.

A new believer is ignorant of the things of God. He is timid regarding his rights in the Kingdom. He lacks experience in spiritual matters. Of course, he should have continual recourse to the anointing that flows from others — from spiritual adults, spiritual fathers. That is only right, and beautiful.

But he must grow up at some point. He must come to spiritual adulthood. Through learning and through experience, he must develop new habits of living. He must learn to live mainly from his own well, not just from the wells of others.

CHAPTER 14

MINISTERING THE ANOINTING
TO AN UNBELIEVER

"In the last days, God says, I will pour out my Spirit ON ALL PEOPLE."
Acts 2:17

For the first couple of years that I gave seminars on the ministry of the Holy Spirit, I dealt exclusively with believers. I ministered the anointing to them, and I taught them how to minister the anointing to other believers.

Then, one day in 1997, while I was in a small town in Colombia, I began to consider the matter of the ministry of the anointing to unbelievers. Could the anointing be ministered to one who was not converted and who possibly even had no wish to be converted? Would the anointing flow forth from me and come upon someone who was, as yet, far from God?

I thought of how the Lord Jesus ministered the Holy Spirit to those as yet not born again — for healings and for deliverance. Could the anointing be ministered to unbelievers for other things too? The Lord reminded me of my own personal experience with the anointing, the first time in my life that the anointing came upon me. It was at a time when I was not yet born again.

One afternoon in 1944, the anointing came upon me as the Spirit of Love. I experienced wave after wave of the flow of the anointing. The love of God was washing over me. It was filling me.

I was very much unsaved at that time. I did not come into the

141

Kingdom until twenty-eight years later. Thus, I knew that the Holy Spirit could manifest Himself to an unbeliever before salvation.

I realized that what had happened to me was a sovereign act of God. He can do as He pleases. What I was thinking of was quite different. Could I, when I wanted to do so, transfer the anointing to an unbeliever, as I had been doing with believers?

As these thoughts and wonderings kept coming to me, I pondered. Was this the Holy Spirit leading me into a new truth? Were these vain speculations? Was this pride and presumption on my part? I prayed for the Lord to clarify my thinking.

When these considerations persisted, I finally decided to experiment in this regard with unsaved people, and I laid the matter at the feet of the Lord for guidance. I asked Him to give me an opportunity to minister the anointing to people who were unsaved and who were not at all open to this ministry before I proposed it to them. I asked the Lord for some "hard cases." I wanted to learn clearly His will in this matter. I had often met unsaved people, whose faces lit up with desire and yearning at the first mention of the ministry of the anointing. "Oh! How I have longed for this for years," they exclaimed. I had always classified these as "easy cases." Using the basketball analogy, it's a "slam-dunk" to minister the anointing to people who are that hungry. I wanted truly hard cases.

"Lord," I prayed, "this is new ground for me. I want to see if I can transfer the anointing to the 'hard cases,' to people who are indifferent to You or even opposed to You. Can I impart the anointing to people who are content in their sins, to people who are not at all interested in You at the moment?"

A few days later, I was eating lunch in the home of one who had been attending the seminar I was giving that week. I remember that day well. The temperature at midday was 44° centigrade (110° Fahrenheit). There was no breeze blowing, and the heat was oppressive.

While I was eating, a man came to the door. He entered and introduced himself to me. He had been in the meeting the night before. He said that he had some friends with him and asked if I would share a word from the Lord with them. They were all politicians from that area, he explained, who had just come from a political business meeting. None of them was a believer.

I was on a missionary trip, and I could hardly afford to pass up an opportunity to share with others what God had given me — whether I was eating or not. So I told him to bring in his friends.

He went out to call his friends from their air-conditioned cars parked in front, and as he was doing this, the Holy Spirit provoked me with these thoughts:

- Nonbelievers and "hard cases" — all!
- Politicians! All wrapped up in their own personal agendas and private interests.
- Fresh from a political meeting, a non-spiritual atmosphere!
- Outside an anointed meeting! In a dining room, with a plate of half-eaten soup in front of me!
- Oppressive heat! Who was in the mood to minister the anointing?
- Hard-core Roman Catholics, with built-in prejudices against non-Catholic ministers!
- In Colombia, where there are hard feelings among traditional Catholics against any evangelistic approach. To take out a Bible or to quote scriptures might immediately "turn them off."

Wow! I thought. This was the ideal time to try what I had been thinking of. Here were the "hard cases" that I had asked the Lord to send my way.

The man returned with his friends in tow and ushered them into the house. There were sixteen of them, both men and women, and each one was more elegantly dressed than the other. It was apparent that they were from the highest social class of the city, all well educated, self-assured and well-to-do. They were individuals whose main interests were the ins and outs of practical politics. Their own personal agendas were uppermost in their minds. All had been born into Roman Catholic families, steeped in the traditions of local Catholic practices and prejudices.

Indeed, the Lord had given me exactly the opportunity to learn the answer to what I had been seeking: Could I minister the anointing to unbelievers in power and see results?

While the visitors were being seated, it came to me to see if I could evangelize nonbelievers through the impact of the anointing upon them, without the use of the Scriptures, as is commonly done.

They were all seated in the living room, which opened up to the dining room, where I was seated, eating my soup, and they all stared at me, as they waited to see what would happen next. I felt awkward sitting before my soup with a spoon in my hand, so I put it down, and stood up to speak with them.

"Our friend here has asked me to say a few words to you regarding what I am doing in your town," I began. "Very simply put, it has to do with this: When I was a teenager, I had a wonderful experience with God that had an effect upon me that has lasted until this present day. He manifested Himself to me personally. He touched me very deeply within. The impact of that experience was something I had never before experienced. It was profound, and it was indelible.

"I realized that Almighty God had taken the time and made the effort to demonstrate to me that He was personally interested in me, just as I was. Actually, at that time, I had no real interest in Him.

"*Señores y Señoras*," I continued in Spanish, "in the years that followed that experience, I have met many people who have remarked to me how much they, too, would value such a personal experience with God, how much they, too, would like to know personally and experientially that God is interested in them. They wish that God would take such action with them, too.

"In these last few years, I have learned how to pray that God give this same blessing to others. I have learned that the Spirit of God is ever willing to show Himself to men and women everywhere. He will demonstrate to them, each one, that He is personally interested in them.

"Without saying anything more, let me make you a simple offer. If you are open and willing that the Holy Spirit manifest Himself to each of you personally, just as you are, then I will pray, and He will show you this right now."

Ministering the Anointing to an Unbeliever

I paused to give them a moment to digest what I had said. Then, one by one, I looked into the eyes of each person and questioned each one personally, "Would you like this demonstration by God, right now?" Each of the sixteen replied in the affirmative.

I asked them all to stand up. Then, I told them to close their eyes and to think only on the Lord Jesus, and to center, to focus, on Him. (Thankfully, Roman Catholics have no problem dealing with thoughts of the Lord Jesus, nor with the power of the Holy Spirit. Their problems often begin with the evangelical barrage of scriptures that many Bible-toting evangelicals lay on them.)

All of the visitors closed their eyes, and then they waited in an attitude of respect. After a few moments, I began to speak very simply with the thoughts of John 7:37-39:

- "Lord Jesus, my sincere desire for these people is that Your Holy Spirit manifest Himself to each one and that each may see personally that You have a unique interest in him.
- Lord, I thank You for Your presence here. In Your presence, I delight. Upon You, I rely.
- Lord Jesus, I am drinking of You, drawing You to myself.
- I believe that, at my words of faith, You will do what You promised — cause the Spirit to flow.

   "Brothers and sisters, what I have I now give you. The Spirit of God now comes upon you to show clearly that He is interested in you personally. In the name of Jesus, receive the anointing right now!"

I passed quickly among them, laying a hand briefly on the head of each. Then I went back to my place, where I remained a few moments in the presence of the Lord, drinking of Him.

In a few moments, I opened my eyes and looked over the sixteen men and women standing before me. They were all motionless. As I looked closer, I could see that they appeared to be in a frozen state. I looked at the sister who had been giving me lunch that day, and at the brother who had brought the group of friends in. We shrugged our shoulders at one another in non-understanding of what was happening. Then, we simply waited for something to happen.

We stayed that way for more than fifteen minutes, and during that time, not one of the sixteen moved a hair. Then, gradually, one by one, they began to open their eyes. They were shaking their heads, acting as if they were coming out of some kind of trance. It was obvious that the Spirit of God had been dealing with each of them during those solemn minutes.

I felt led to say to the group: "Now you have seen, in your own experience, that God, the Lord Jesus, is personally interested in you just as you are. He has shown you this. It is His presence within you that has left you with this wonderful sense of peace that He always gives when He manifests Himself to a person. So, now, I come to this second offer I have for you.

"Would each of you like to be able to enjoy often these things that God has just shown you? You can have this deep peace every day of your life if you want. I will pray again, and this time the Spirit of God will take up residence in each of your hearts if you so choose. If you do, you will always have the delights that come from His indwelling presence."

Again I looked at each one in turn with this question. This time they were more certain. "Certainly," they all agreed. "Who wouldn't want this always?"

I explained to them that, for this peace and presence of God to be a permanent reality, each and every one of them would have to pray sincerely for pardon from their sins. They would have to renounce sinful habits. They would have to accept the Lord Jesus as their personal Savior and as Lord of their lives. They were to invite the Lord into their lives, and He would come to them. Then, they were to pray with me to the Lord that He fill each with the Holy Spirit. The Spirit would then come to reside in them. They all agreed that this was what they wanted.

I led them in the sinner's prayer and in the asking for and the receiving of the baptism of the Holy Spirit. Again I passed among them, briefly touching the head of each. Then I returned to my original place.

146

Ministering the Anointing to an Unbeliever

Once more, all of the visitors appeared to be lost in another world. This time it lasted for about eight to ten minutes. Then, they came out of their rapt state, all deeply overcome by what had just happened. They began to share, joyfully, with each other what they had just experienced.

I spoke a bit more to the group about what had happened to them. I told them of their need to learn more about the new Treasure that was now within them. I explained their need for the spiritual food from the Word of God and their need to meet regularly with other believers.

They agreed that they needed to learn more and that they wanted to do so. They decided to meet together in a house as a group, with the brother who had brought them to lead them in the things of the Lord. They wanted more of the intimate presence of the Lord to which they had just been introduced.

As the group began to leave, they thanked me profusely. They were all marveling joyfully at what had happened to them. As one very refined and elegantly dressed woman passed me, she gushed in joy and delight, "Never in my entire life have I ever experienced a marvel such as this!" Later, I was told that she was the richest woman in the city.

How delighted I was! I now knew that the anointing could be imparted to nonbelievers with a powerful impact, and to evangelize them, too.

The next day, the brother who had brought the politicians to me sought me out. "Albert," he said. "Do you know what happened to them while they were 'frozen' under the anointing?"

I said, "No, I haven't the foggiest idea."

He went on, " While they were under that heavy anointing, each one of them had the same vision. Each saw tongues of fire over the heads of everyone in the room. And all felt a strong wind blowing through the room. The clothes of all were moving under the power of the wind."

They had each experienced the same things that had happened on the Day of Pentecost in Acts 2. Now, I really had my answer from the Lord regarding the ministry of the anointing to unbelievers. He had answered me with a resounding, "ABSOLUTELY AND POSITIVELY,

YES! I want My Spirit poured out on ALL flesh — saved and unsaved alike!"

I need to point out that I am not an evangelist. My service to the Body of Christ has always been that of teaching the Word of God to believers. However, from that day until now, as I go about teaching seminars on how to minister the anointing, a part of what I cover in detail is always the ministry of the anointing to evangelize unbelievers.

That experience changed my life. Ever since that day, as I begin a seminar in a church on a Sunday morning, I put this to the congregation:

"Brothers and sisters, during this week that I am with your church, I need invitations to your houses or to your places of business. I need some of you to invite me to come to talk to your friends, to your neighbors, to your relatives and to your employees. I want you to invite people who are not saved. Tell them to come for a luncheon or for tea and cake in the afternoon. Do not say that you are inviting them to a religious meeting. Tell them that it will be a simple meeting, in friendship, for them to learn something of great interest and value to them. Tell them that you want them to meet a friend of yours who is traveling through this week. That friend, of course, is me."

During a week of seminar in a church, I will typically have six to ten such meetings, and in each one anywhere from six to fifty unsaved people will attend. One woman went all over her neighborhood inviting people to attend, and a hundred and twenty-five came. We had to go outside into the street to hold our session. Every one of those accepted my invitation, and they became permanent temples of the Spirit.

To date, two to three thousand people have come to Christ in response to this simple invitation. The offers I make are the same as in that first meeting, with none of the customary overtones of modern evangelistic methods. So far, only eight people have refused the offers. Six of those did accept the first offer, of learning that God was personally interested in them. These six said that they were not yet ready to make a commitment to the Lord Jesus.

Thus, it has become a common occurrence for me to come into a church of from a hundred and fifty to two hundred and fifty members, and after the meetings with unbelievers in the houses, to leave behind at the end of the week one hundred brand-new converts, all baptized with the Holy Spirit.

I most certainly do not have a unique gift to evangelize by the anointing. As I have said, I have *"the gift of God,"* the Holy Spirit. ANY-ONE and EVERYONE who has this gift can do what I do.

After I show the leaders in a couple of meetings what I am doing, I have them lead other similar meetings. The results are always the same, and the fruit of this ministry continues to come in long after I have gone.

Let me emphasize the obvious here. This is ministry of the anointing outside of programmed religious meetings. This is part of the out-working of the promise of God to pour forth His Spirit upon all flesh. This is a response to the cry of the Lord Jesus to ANYONE, to every member of His Body, to minister the anointing. The Holy Spirit did not come into believers to be shut up within the walls of a building we call a church.

The Holy Spirit is not fragile, needing protection from nonreligious surroundings. In the Old Testament, did not the Ark of the Covenant, which contained the presence of the Lord, go before His people into battle? This world belongs to our God. His rightful place is every-where, especially where He is yet not received. He has given the anointing to believers that we may bring Him everywhere we go. He does not wish to remain closed up within us. Rather, we are to ever seek opportunities to have Him show Himself by the anointing we can minister to others.

What Christianity has done over the centuries is to forget the ex-amples of the manifestations of the anointing that are presented in the book of Acts. There, the Holy Spirit is shown manifesting Himself out-side planned religious meetings. He never closed Himself up in a church building. There were no church buildings until centuries later.

The Holy Spirit has been sent to draw unbelievers to the Lord Jesus. Where do we find such people? They are outside of our church build-ings. They are outside of planned religious meetings.

The Lord is continually demonstrating to me that He wants all be-lievers to impart the Holy Spirit to others. This includes people who will never choose to come to a church meeting, or even to a crusade in a stadium. There are countless people everywhere who will never come in contact with an ordained minister. We must reach out to them wherever we find them.

Such people are continually in contact with "ordinary" believers like you and me, and we have the anointing within us. The Lord is waiting for us to cause Him to flow forth to touch everyone whom we know. Through us, He wants to touch those who have never experienced Him. He can reach them only if we take time to share with them that which is so precious to each of us. We must take advantage of every opportunity to do this. If need be, we must make opportunities to do it.

Think about what God is showing us here. There are multiplied millions in the world who do not yet know Him, and have never experienced Him. All of them, however, seem to be willing to have a "taste" of Him, to "sample" Him. They would truly love to know personally that God is interested in them individually. And a believer can present the Lord to anyone — a personal introduction.

It is one thing to present our Lord by His Word (and in no way am I putting down the Word and its power). But it is another dimension altogether to present to people, personally, the God of the Word.

In my little extra-church meetings, I have had many extremely traditional Christian religious people, committed Muslims, idolaters and even atheists. The striking example that stands out in my mind is that of a man who came with a group of thirty or so to whom I made my offer. All of them but him quickly accepted the offer to see if God was truly interested in each of them individually. With a tolerant smile on his face, this man raised his hand politely. "Sir," he said, "this is all very well and good for the others here. But this is not for me. You see, I am an atheist. I do not believe that any god exists. I do not believe that Jesus is God."

As I looked at him, I sensed the softness of the Spirit upon me, and I began to answer him, accordingly. "Very well. You do not believe that God exists. You do not believe that Jesus is God. I will make no attempt to persuade you to the contrary. But think for a moment of the possibility that you may not be right.

"Just in case God might really exist, just in case Jesus might be God,

150

Ministering the Anointing to an Unbeliever

just in case He might want to reveal Himself to you, wouldn't it be to your advantage to know that now, while you are on the earth, instead of learning these things are true after you pass on to the next world? You have nothing to lose if you let me pray for you regarding this offer, and it seems to me that you have everything to gain. If the Lord Jesus does show you that He exists and that He is interested in you, you gain, for you will have learned a truth that is valuable to you. If, on the other hand, nothing happens when I pray for you, you have the chance to laugh at me and call me a clown.

"So, what do you say now? All you need is a simple openness, an 'in case You do exist' thinking. Simply say, 'Jesus, I do not believe that You exist. But if You do, I am open that You show me.'"

He thought for a few seconds. Then he smiled and shrugged his shoulders. "Fine," he said, "I am open to see."

I ministered the anointing to everyone present, and they all "froze" in the Spirit, including the confessed atheist.

After ten minutes or so, they began to open their eyes, and I made the second offer (salvation and the Spirit to reside permanently within each one of them). I looked into the eyes of the avowed atheist and asked him, "Do you want this? Do you want permanently what you just experienced?"

"Yes, I do," he said with alacrity and joy. The rest readily agreed with him. And so they all came to the Lord for salvation, and all of them received the baptism of the Spirit.

After a few minutes, I asked the group if they would like to see that each them could now do what I had just done with them. Because the Holy Spirit now resided in them in the same way He resided in me, they could minister the anointing also. As I was saying this, I was looking directly at my new brother, the former atheist. He laughed with joy. Clapping his hands, he exclaimed, "Of course I do. Show me how!"

I then went on to teach them all the instructions of our Lord in John 7:37-39. I had them lay hands on one another, and the anointing flowed. Each of them was now a minister of the anointing. What a turn of events! Ten minutes after a man's public profession of atheism, he was now saved and ministering the anointing to others.

Consider the number of people alive on the earth today. One estimate says that there are between seven and eight billion men and women alive today. Of those, probably less than ten percent are born-again Christians. So, here we are, nearly two thousand years after the Lord gave the command to His Body, the Church, to go forth to bring conversion to all. Yet today there are far more unsaved than saved, billions more. Can these results be considered successful compliance with the Lord's command?

I do not presume to judge anyone, yet I cannot but be impacted by a few obvious facts. During the past generations, the Church has offered salvation to the unsaved by means of preaching. Sinners have been invited to our church buildings to hear our preaching. They have been invited to large evangelistic crusades. Some have preached the Word on street corners or in other public places, and others have gone out knocking on doors to share it.

But the ministry of the anointing has been very limited. It has been limited to church buildings or to private meetings of believers. Only a very few men, relatively speaking, in the whole world have been actively ministering the anointing. That has been reserved for those we call ordained ministers, men to whom we give titles, "Reverend So-and-So," "Pastor So-and-So" or "Doctor So-and-So." These practices of centuries have produced only the minimal results that we see today.

In truth, the class of believers we have come to call "ministers" do not even have ready access to the billions of unsaved in the world. They deal mainly with planned meetings — in church buildings or stadiums — meetings to which most of the unsaved billions will never come. But there are many millions of us ordinary believers who have the anointing within us. We do have access to the billions of unsaved. We meet them every day as we go about our daily activities.

It is the millions of Holy Spirit anointed believers who can do what the Lord has shown me must be done. I have already shown hundreds of others how to do it, and they are doing it on their own. Now we need millions of anointed believers who can minister the anointing to touch the billions of unbelievers.

Millions of anointed believers can introduce the Lord Jesus personally to unbelievers through ministering the anointing to them. Millions of believers can evangelize by sharing the person and presence of the God of the Word.

The Word of God promises that in the last days the Spirit will be poured forth upon all flesh. How is this to be accomplished? Will it be a sudden raining down from Heaven as was the case on the Day of Pentecost? We'll let God be God in how He fulfills His promises. But, let us also take full advantage of what God has already done. The Spirit has already been poured forth into the world. He is here, now, and ready for action.

How can we continue to look up to the clouds for what we already have with us? God has taken up residence within us.

Now, in this last and greatest move of the Spirit before the coming of the Lord, there will be millions of believers ministering the anointing all over the earth. The Lord tells me that this is a part of His plan to pour out the Spirit on all flesh.

The Spirit of the Lord gives deep witness to me of this: When the Lord Jesus baptized me with the Spirit, He ordained me as a minister of the anointing. He was enabling me, and constituting me as His agent, to bring forth the anointing to impact others. I am anointed, and therefore I can minister the anointing to others.

Brother, Sister, do you not have the same Holy Spirit witness within you? Let us all go out from our private meetings to lay hands on everyone around us. Let us develop the habit of behavior that Peter learned early in his Christian experience: "What I have, I give you. Receive the anointing for your needed provision."

This ministry is for ANYONE and EVERYONE, especially when outside church buildings and outside planned meetings.

CHAPTER 15

SOME FINAL OBSERVATIONS

I have a few final observations that I trust will be helpful:

REGARDING PLACE

The anointing may be ministered to people who are with, or in the same physical place as, the person ministering. But the Spirit may also be ministered to those who are not present at the time of the ministering. We may minister the anointing over the telephone, over the radio, over television and over the Internet.

The Holy Spirit does not need connecting lines through which to flow. He is just as much present where the receiving person is as where the ministering person is. Although He has chosen to minister through people and we are in fixed places, He is God and God is everywhere.

As with those to whom you minister in person, prepare those who are on the receiving end of the telephone or e-mail. Tell them what their part is so that they may receive the anointing. As they are obedient, the anointing will come upon them as the Spirit is ministered.

THE MINISTRY OF THE ANOINTING TO PEOPLE WHO ARE UNAWARE OF SUCH MINISTRY

The anointing can be ministered to people who are not present and can even be ministered to those who are not aware that it is being done. The one ministering the anointing will sense power going forth from him.

Some Final Observations

For example: Are you single? Do you have within you a deep desire that the Lord give you the mate that He has chosen for you (even though you may not have met that person yet)? The person God has for you is alive at this moment, and although you may not know who that person is, God obviously does. The Spirit is present wherever that person may be.

Place your hands upon your own belly. Close your eyes and begin to minister the anointing to that person (as yet unknown to you):

Lord Jesus, I desire deeply to marry the person You have chosen for me.
Into Your presence I now come. I rest in You.
I drink of You, Lord, so that the anointing will flow to come upon this person
— for salvation, if necessary, for preparation for our marriage and for the
plan You have for us in life. Bring us together, Lord.
I believe that You are doing this now by Your Spirit.
In the name of Jesus, the anointing goes forth from me now to do these things.

Then, wait in the presence of the Lord, as you continue drinking of Him. You will sense the anointing welling up within you as He shows you that He is now setting out to do according to your words. Continue ministering in this manner each day ... until the blessing comes to you.

REGARDING THE TIME THAT MAY ELAPSE BEFORE THE BLESSING COMES

Sometimes, the anointing is ministered and the desired result comes about right away, or at least very soon. But sometimes it does not come so soon. The prayer of faith works in this way, and so, too, does ministry of the anointing. In each situation, the Lord has His reasons and purposes regarding the time span that passes before the sought blessing comes. Keep believing. It will come.

My experience is this: I minister the anointing for something I desire. Right then, I sense the flow of the anointing. When the blessing does not appear immediately, I keep on ministering the anointing daily, even more than once a day. I do this until the blessing comes. This goes equally for ministry to myself and ministry to others.

An example of this may be ministry of the anointing to a non-Christian mate, even one who has been difficult or harsh to the believing spouse. In one of my meetings, a woman heard this and decided to put it to the test. She was married to an unsaved man, and he had been strongly opposing her Christian practices. It had gotten to the point that he was now harsh toward her. He was developing habits that were very harmful to the marriage.

She listened carefully that night as I explained how she could minister the Spirit to her unsaved husband. She decided that she would try it that very night, while he was asleep at her side.

When she got back home, she found that her husband was still out. She went to bed alone, and after tossing and turning for a long while, she finally fell asleep. Her husband eventually came home and immediately came into their bedroom. He was drunk. As he stumbled around the room, she was awakened. Still fully clothed, he fell into the bed and was immediately asleep.

After a few minutes, the woman decided to go ahead with her plan to minister the anointing to him. She laid her hands on him and expressed her heart desires for him according to John 7:37-39. The anointing came forth from her immediately, and her husband sat up sharply in the bed. "What was that shock that just went through me?" he cried.

"Oh, nothing, dear," she answered. "I think it was only God showing you that He is blessing you. Just go back to sleep." He lay back down and went to sleep.

That next night, the woman testified in the meeting about what had happened. She said she would continue ministering the Spirit to her husband every night. She knew that the Spirit was now actively at work on his behalf.

How long should you continue such ministry before you can expect to see the desired result? There is no rule. Keep doing it until the result appears.

REGARDING THE ONE MINISTERING THE ANOINTING SENSING THE ANOINTING FLOW OUT

I sense the flowing out of the anointing as I minister the Spirit to others. The delights of such sensings are beyond telling. It is a blessing which awaits all believers who will come into the ministry of the anointing.

There are also times, however, in the ministry of the anointing when I do not sense the flowing out as I go through the steps of John 7:37-39. I remember the times when I first experienced such "non-sensings" of the flow of the Spirit. Doubts came to me that the anointing had gone forth. In such cases, I asked the ones receiving, "Did you sense the anointing right now?"

"Oh, yes," they always answered. "The anointing came upon me wonderfully!"

It still happens once in a while, but I have learned not to seek confirmation that the anointing flowed when I did not feel it. Experience had shown me that it has indeed gone forth — always as I have ministered according to John 7:37-39. Therefore, there is no reason to seek confirmation from others. My part is to do what the Lord said to do, and His part is to see to it that the results take place as He said they would. He is faithful to His Word.

Actually, some of the most noteworthy things that I have seen done through the ministry of the anointing have happened when I sensed nothing during the ministering.

As regards a person who is receiving the anointing, I find that it is very rare that he does not sense the anointing when the Spirit is ministered to him. In general, I believe that when a person comes forward with an open, honest heart, he will sense the anointing come upon him.

I have experienced a couple of cases where the people involved needed deliverance from demonic influences in their lives before the anointing was manifested to them. But I cannot say that this would be so in all cases. I am merely putting forth what I have seen in my limited experience.

REGARDING THE FOUR HEART ACTIVITIES OF JOHN 7:37-39

As I have said, when I am ministering the anointing in meetings anywhere, I go through these four matters one by one. I clearly define each point. I do this especially because I am demonstrating to everyone present the teaching of the Lord in these verses. I want them all to understand clearly how to do what I do. It is usually new to those who are listening.

Practically all of the people I minister to have never before ministered the anointing. They are seeking plain, direct teaching on the subject. They want to understand all that they are called to do to minister in like manner. For the sake of teaching simplicity, I go over these points slowly, as I show how the anointing will flow from one who does what the Lord says. I want the people to know the fundamentals of this ministry.

At other times, however, the circumstances are different, and I do not methodically go through the four points. After many months of ministering the anointing, it becomes second nature to be involved with all four of them at the same time.

Also, I find that at times I will be concentrating on one of these heart attitudes much more than on the other three. Still, the anointing flows.

THE MINISTRY OF THE ANOINTING TO ONE PERSON OR TO MANY AT THE SAME TIME

I minister the anointing to one person or to hundreds at the same time, and the anointing flows upon all of them. There is no difference.

The anointing also flows forth to others with or without the laying on of my hands. Sometimes, when I cannot physically reach everyone who is present because of the crowded space, God works anyway.

The important thing is for me to have faith in the words of the Lord in John 7:37-39. A person ministering the anointing must be fully given over in faith to the teachings of these verses.

The people who would receive the anointing need to be open to receiving. Faith on their part in the words of the Lord will also be of great help at this time, but it is not imperative that they be physically touched by the one ministering.

The anointing, after all, is the work of the Spirit, and He can always reach all men everywhere.

Part III

Conclusions

CHAPTER 16

THE STATE OF THE MINISTRY OF THE ANOINTING IN THE BODY OF CHRIST AT PRESENT AND INTO THE FUTURE

In Part I of this book, there is analysis of the teaching of the Lord Jesus regarding the ministry of the anointing. He said that ANYONE may minister the anointing. On the night just before He died, He stated that the anointing would be of great benefit to those who believed on Him once He had gone to be with His Father. From then on, He would send the Holy Spirit to dwell within men and women so that they might do the marvelous things He had done, and even greater things.

When Jesus walked the earth, He was the only person alive who had the anointing of the Spirit residing permanently within Him. Now, that was to change. Such a blessing was to be for all His followers. Jesus' concept of the Body of Christ, therefore, was that all its members would act just as He had under the anointing.

The ministry of Jesus had brought blessings to many people, but it had also served to demonstrate what would be happening in the lives of all of His followers afterward.

Obviously, this is not being done today by many of the members of Christ's Body. What He taught us to do, what He expected us to do and what He looked forward to the Spirit doing through us is not being done by the vast majority of His followers.

ONE REASON FOR THIS FAILURE

A chief cause of the lack of widespread ministry of the anointing is the acceptance that there are two classes of believers. One is called "the clergy," and the other is called "the laity." Today, as has been the case for centuries, we find that there exists a division in the Body of Christ. This division has been promoted and prolonged until it has become accepted tradition. Church leaders have acted as if there was a special class of believers who are the constituted ministers of the power of the Holy Spirit, and they have taught others that this is so. Some believers go through lengthy preparation in order to be recognized as ministers by others, and once they have finished this preparation, they are known as "clergymen." All other believers are expected to be receivers of the ministry of the clergymen.

There are a number of problems with this tradition. The first is that it is men who decide which certain few will be designated as those who minister to the multiplied millions of those who are not so ordained. The result is that the great majority of believers have accepted for themselves something that their Lord never intended for them — a lifetime of looking to a few for the manifesting of the power of God when they need it. They are reduced to traveling to a place where there is someone who might cause the power of the anointing to come into their lives. In the meantime, they live in a state of lack with regard to the very real needs they have.

This is sad, for within every Spirit-filled believer is the very Treasure he or she has grown accustomed to seeking after from another. Too many seek to draw from the well in another, when all the while they have a full well of their own within themselves. They have never been taught by their leaders to draw living water from their own wells. They have never been taught to bring forth rivers of living water to all the people they know who so sorely need it.

It is true that we are being told that we are members of the Body of Christ, the Anointed One, but we are not being told that the same anointing He had now abides in us. So, many Christians live out their Christian lives as powerless members of His Body. They are called by the very Head of the Body to cause the anointing to flow out from themselves to others, but they never come to the place where He can use them in the earth in this way. This ministry of the anointing has been given by the Lord to all of His followers. It is for ANY and ALL who have themselves been anointed with the Spirit.

When the Lord gives the Holy Spirit to a believer, He Himself is doing the ordaining. By anointing a human being with the Holy Spirit, the Lord Jesus is constituting that person as a minister of the anointing. When He baptizes a person with the Holy Spirit, that person then has the Spirit of God within him. No one has more of the Spirit of God than he has.

The Spirit of God is a person, and when He chooses to dwell within a man or a woman, He is just as much with that person as He is with anyone else in the world. He is ready to flow forth from that person, from any person, to do His works in the earth. No man who has been ordained of men has more of the Holy Spirit than a person who has not received that ordination.

What many "ordained" ministers do have is experience in ministering the anointing. Some of them have been ministering the anointing for thirty, forty or even fifty years. Marvels are being done by the Spirit through them in ever-increasing measure. The more a person ministers the Spirit, the more the Spirit will do through that willing and cooperating agent.

But all of those who now actively minister the anointing had to start somewhere. They had a first time, and they went on from there. They began by seeing a little fruit through their ministrations. Increase came over time, and it came because of their continual ministry. If we can have millions of believers all over the earth in the coming years doing what the Lord has called and enabled ANYONE and EVERYONE to do, they will be glorious years — for the Anointed One, the Christ, and for His Body of active members. All believers should be seeing God moving through them in continually increasing measure. Unbelievers would be impacted by seeing the Gospel of Christ demonstrated in the earth.

What has resulted from the practice of only the man-ordained ministers ministering the anointing is the present powerless state of the Church. Each new believer dutifully takes his place among the laity.

He is not a minister, and unless and until he can fulfill certain conditions set down by the group, he can never hope to be recognized as such. Conversion should be the moment that we recognize every man and woman as ministers and begin to train them in that capacity. What the Lord has said in John 7:37-39 is rarely considered where the ministry of the anointing is concerned.

The consequences to the human race of just a few ministering the anointing is lamentable. What has resulted is that there are many millions of people on the earth who have never been touched by the anointing of the Holy Spirit. The few constituted ministers who do minister the anointing form a puny number when we consider the billions who are in need. It will take many millions to do the work in the days ahead, and thank God, He is anointing millions to do it.

If every believer who is being blessed with *"the gift of God"* could be taught what the Lord has enabled him to do, and if men and women were continually encouraged and exhorted to go forth in their Christ-ordained ministry, what a difference we could make in the human race.

I know we are talking about "nobodies," but God has chosen to anoint nobodies to minister the anointing. If each of us were to become alert to the needs around us and to the opportunities we have all around us to minister the Holy Spirit, to lift burdens and to destroy oppressions, what a different world this would be. Is not this what our Lord always intended for us? As time passes, and the activity of the anointing increases through each one of us, will not the knowledge of the glory of the Lord cover the earth as the waters cover the sea — just as He has promised?

OTHER PORTIONS OF SCRIPTURE TO CONSIDER ON THIS MATTER

1. *"And he gave some, apostles; and some, prophets; and some, evangelists; and some, pastors and teachers; for the perfecting of the saints, FOR THE WORK OF THE MINISTRY... ,"* (Ephesians 4:11-12, KJV). Those in the Body of Christ who have special offices to perform are certainly called to a unique service. The Holy Spirit will do things through them that He does not do through

others. But, here, we are told that one of their chief responsibilities is to prepare all believers FOR THE WORK OF THE MINISTRY. They are not told that only they are to do the ministering, while the large majority never does more than receive from them. THE LEADERS AMONG US ARE CALLED TO SHOW THE REST OF US HOW TO DO WHAT THEY ARE DOING. They are called to develop all believers to do what the Lord expects of all members of His Body. One of His expectations and desires is that ANYONE and EVERYONE minister the anointing to do the things for which He has given them the Spirit.

2. To the Church in Ephesus: *"But you have this in your favor: You hate the practices of the Nicolaitans, which I also hate"* (Revelation 2:6). To the Church in Pergamum: *"Nevertheless, I have a few things against you: You have people there who hold to the teaching of Balaam, who taught Balak to entice the Israelites to sin by eating food sacrificed to idols and by committing sexual immorality. Likewise you also have those who hold to the teaching of the Nicolaitans. Repent therefore! Otherwise, I will soon come to you and will fight against them with the sword of my mouth"* (Revelation 2:14-16). These are strong words from the Lord Jesus. For a long time, I wondered just what the practices of the Nicolaitans the Lord hated so had been. I could not seem to find any explanation. Then, a short time ago, a friend came to me with a startling revelation. He had become concerned regarding the way the ministry of the anointing had been reserved for a man-chosen few. Leaders in his church had set limits regarding who was permitted to minister the anointing. Laypersons and children were being restricted from participating in such activity. He told me that the Lord had led him to these two portions of scripture in Revelation 2. Then, the Lord led him to break the word Nicolaitans into two parts and look up each part in a Greek dictionary.

What he found was that *nikos* means "suppressing, " and *laikos* means "laypeople, those not officially designated as ministers." It seemed to him, therefore, that the thing the Lord hated so much was the suppression of laypeople. As far back as the first century, there had arisen a doctrine of separation of clergy and laity. Already, there was a class of ordained ministers who were reserving to themselves the activities of ministry. People were learning to come to them for needed ministry. These leaders were not teaching everyone else to do what they had learned to do. They were reserving the ministry of the power of the Spirit to themselves.

The Holy Spirit thus showed my friend that the wrongful division between ordained ministers and laity had begun very early in the Church. Very early, the Body of Christ was being divided into the ministers of the power and the receivers of the power. Plainly, this was never the intention of the Lord. This went directly against His teaching that ANYONE could, and EVERYONE should, minister the anointing.

This wrong teaching infuriated the Lord Jesus, and He said, *"You have this in your favor: You hate the practices of the Nicolaitans, which I also hate."* He intends the ministry of the anointing to be done by ALL believers. He hates anything that prevents His ANYONEs from ministering the anointing, so that the works of God can be done through them.

A VISION THAT CONFIRMS IT

I love the vision the Lord gave to one of His servants in 1961. The man received the same vision in the same detail again in 1981. Although the vision was not given to me directly by the Lord, it has, nevertheless, burned within me since the first time I heard it. The Spirit of the Lord has so impacted me with this vision that it has long ago become my vision. It is this vision that motivates me in the work I do to spread the teachings of this book.

The vision began with a panoramic scene of the whole earth. It was presented on a flat plane. The earth was shown as a vast map, with all the continents, countries, islands and seas stretched forth upon it. Sprawled across the great expanse of the map, there lay an immense giant. His body was so great that it extended over the entire expanse of the map. His head, trunk, arms, legs and feet extended out in every direction and covered the earth. Part of the giant was lying upon every continent and upon every great body of water.

The massive giant, lying lazily over the whole world, was doing nothing more than existing. He appeared to have no desire and little or no strength to do anything but lie where he was. He was dressed shabbily, and he was dirty and unkempt.

As the vision continued, there were highlighted hordes of small creatures crawling all over the body of the giant. They were hideous, filthy and disgusting beings, and they could be seen entering and exiting from him at will because of the unconcern and lack of unawareness exhibited by the lazy giant.

This scene continued for a while. Then, suddenly, the giant moved a bit. He moved his arms, lifted his head and chest and stirred his body. As he did this, thousands of the little, hideous creatures began to flee.

Very shortly, the giant fell back into his former lazy position and again did nothing. When this happened, the ugly little creatures flocked back and began to infest him. Soon, they were having their unopposed will with him again.

This scene repeated itself several times. There was a bit of activity on the part of the giant, a fleeing of the ugly creatures. Then when the giant returned to his lethargic state, it was followed by the storming back of thousands of the ugly creatures to pollute him all over again.

After a little while, something new began to happen. From the clouds overhead, there began to fall tiny droplets of what appeared to be liquid light. These shiny droplets fell upon the giant in his dirty, lazy, infested condition. As they fell upon him, they began to have an immediate effect. He began to move his legs and arms again. Gradually, his entire body began to move. As it did, hordes of the ugly creatures that had been crawling over him began to leave him. Many that had been within him came forth and departed.

Soon, the giant rose to a sitting position. The fall of the droplets of liquid light did not cease. It began to increase, and the droplets became larger. The falling liquid light began to wash over him. Then, mustering his great strength, he rose to his feet. The ugly creatures were now freely flowing out from his body, and they were fleeing from him in panic.

After a while, the massive giant lifted up his arms to the heavens. They extended up through the clouds. He was giving thanks to the Lord and praising Him with all his heart.

Soon, a strange thing began to happen to the praising giant. The liquid light was now pouring down upon him in torrents. In that downpour, the giant began to melt, even as a figure carved in the sand at the seashore is washed away as the waves come upon it. He continued melting away in that flow of liquid light until he had totally disappeared. What had been a massive giant was now absorbed into the earth upon which he had been standing.

Then, there began to sprout up, all over the earth, in every country of the world, small individuals, multitudes of them — everywhere. Whereas, before, there had been one great giant, in his place there were now millions of small people. They appeared in every country, on every island and even over the seas.

The liquid drops of light now increased again, and they flowed copiously over these people who were everywhere in the earth. The people began to move about in the lands where they were. As they did, the same liquid light that had come upon them began to flow out from each of them, as they sought out other people. They, themselves, had each become a source for the flow of this wondrous liquid light.

Physical healings of all sorts were caused by the liquid light flowing from them. Through the ministering of the millions, astonishing things were happening. Limbs were appearing where formerly there had been none; eyes, where before there had been none. All manner of sicknesses, diseases, deformities and distortion was healed by the liquid light. This was happening in untold numbers all over the earth. The people in the earth who were not sources of the liquid light were being greatly impacted by what the liquid light was doing.

As this panorama of healing power continued, there were seen some people in the earth who were withdrawing themselves from the liquid light and its miraculous activity. They drew back from it and gradually faded away into darkness, forever separated from its blessed workings.

The State of the Ministry of the Anointing in the Body of Christ

Still, great signs and wonders increased — healings, miracles, marvels of all sorts — everywhere. The liquid light continued to flow forth with great power to bless every area of the lives of men and women who were being touched by it, and all these things were happening through the ministry of millions of seemingly insignificant individuals.

Then, suddenly, the Lord Jesus Himself appeared as a great figure in the heavens. He extended His hand to one part of the earth, and as He did this, there was an instant deluge of liquid light to that area. He extended His hand toward another land, then another, and then another, and always the result was a great flow of liquid light to the area He was focusing on.

This brought on a time of widespread evangelization. The millions from whom flowed the liquid light in power began to impact many other millions, and these millions accepted their message. They, in turn, were filled with the liquid light, and they, too, became dispensers of the liquid light to multitudes of others. Thus, many millions more became filled with the liquid light.

As the vision continued, hardship and persecution began to appear for those who were engaged in the activity of liquid light. These persecutions were strong, but the liquid light was seen to be protecting and comforting those involved with it.

Then, another great change began taking place. The multiplied millions who were now filled with the liquid light began to melt. They began to fade away into the earth, even as had happened to the great giant earlier. All of these millions gradually melted and disappeared into the ground.

Just as the last of the people had disappeared, the giant again began to rise up out from the earth. He grew to be even greater than his former immense size. His head and shoulders now reached up through the clouds.

The change in his appearance was marvelous. He was clean, and his skin glowed with robust health. He was clothed in gleaming, white clothing. He was truly *"without spot or wrinkle."* His arms were lifted high over the clouds, in worship, and he was singing praises and adoration to the Lord.

Then, the Lord Jesus reappeared in the heavens. He was looking lovingly at this beautiful giant from whom there radiated the liquid light.

Jesus was smiling at him. Then the Lord spoke out, "This is truly My Bride. Come up here with Me!"

The giant lifted off from the earth and rose up to be at the side of the Lord. Then, they both disappeared into the heavens.

This glorious vision of the Body of Christ and the activity of the Holy Spirit through His Body speaks of what is to happen before the Lord Jesus comes for His Bride. It speaks of the present spiritual condition of the members of the Body — the moral uncleanness, the laziness and ineffectiveness as regards the purpose given to us by our Head. It speaks of the present lack of activity of Holy Spirit power through the members of the Body.

But, thank God, the vision was not all negative. It also speaks of a great change that will come over the members of the Body of Christ worldwide. The Spirit will move on all members in measures of divine power never before seen — for cleansing, for holiness, for great miracles, for signs and wonders. Evangelism in the power of the Holy Spirit will be an awesome work of God through His people.

As I have said, in recent years I have had the opportunity to minister on three continents, and everywhere I have gone, I have found many members of the Body of Christ in the same spiritual condition as the giant of this vision, as he was first presented. Most of them are not engaged in the ministry of the anointing.

In the past couple of years, however, I have been seeing something new. God's liquid light is beginning to fall on His people, and the results are clearly visible. Those who have received this touch of liquid light are going forth to cause it to come upon others. There are many supernatural results.

I am convinced that I am seeing the beginning of what the vision foretold — millions of members of the Body of Christ receiving the anointing. They are being cleansed. All former demonic influences in their lives are gone. And they are going forth boldly all over the world to do the final work of the Lord in the great power of the Spirit. All this must be accomplished before the closing of the age. As the Lord has promised, the knowledge of the glory of the Lord will fill the earth, even as the waters cover the sea. Then, the Lord will summon His Bride to Himself!

The State of the Ministry of the Anointing in the Body of Christ

To me, this vision expresses clearly the current state of the Body of Christ — and the future. Occasionally, the Holy Spirit quickens the vision to me, and I see parts of it unfolding. Already, there are thousands who have learned to minister the anointing. These are ordinary people, nobodies, as regards renown. They have learned to go forward in this ministry, as they experience the flow of Holy Spirit power.

The vision speaks of what ANYONE can and will do as he or she takes literally what the Lord has said in John 7:37-39. The vision speaks of the time when all who know how to minister the anointing will be busily doing it, and busily teaching others to do what they have learned to do. It speaks of millions of ANYONEs at work, to the glory of the Anointed One, their Head.

A FINAL EXHORTATION

I have to wonder what the impact of this vision might have been if it had come to Paul in his day. He exhorted Timothy to minister the anointing continually when that young man was a ministerial nobody. Timothy had received the anointing for Holy Spirit power, but was doing nothing with it. Paul wrote to him:

> *I thank God, whom I serve, as my forefathers did, with a clear conscience, as night and day I constantly remember you in my prayers. Recalling your tears, I long to see you, so that I may be filled with joy. I have been reminded of your sincere faith, which first lived in your grandmother Lois and in your mother Eunice and, I am persuaded, now lives in you also. For this reason I remind you to fan into flame the gift of God, which is in you through the laying on of my hands. For God did not give us a spirit of timidity, but a spirit of power, of love and of self-discipline.*
> *So do not be ashamed to testify about our Lord, or ashamed of me his prisoner. But join with me in suffering for the gospel, by the power of God, who has saved us and called us to a holy life — not because of anything we have done but because of his own purpose and grace. This grace was given us in Christ Jesus before the beginning of time. ...*
> *You then, my son, be strong in the grace that is in Christ Jesus.*
>
> 2 Timothy 1:3-9 and 2:1

When Paul first ministered to Timothy, he taught him the things of the Kingdom of God. The young man responded with sincere faith in the words Paul shared with him. This is the kind of faith one needs in order that he might have the activity of the anointing through him. He must exercise sincere faith, putting it to work in the daily opportunities of his living situation.

One must act upon this faith. For, unless a believer does his part so that the Holy Spirit flows through him, God cannot demonstrate the anointing in the earth through that believer. Unless a believer takes positive steps to cause his faith to arise within him, he will not see the Spirit act through him to accomplish the work. Sincere faith will cause the anointing to flow.

In verse 6, Paul was saying, "Timothy, I laid my hands on you. The Holy Spirit, the anointing with divine power, came into you. He took up residence within you. The Lord Jesus personally gave to you *'the gift of God,'* the greatest gift the Creator can bestow on one of His creatures. Divinity came to dwell within you.

"But, Timothy, you have been doing nothing with this great gift. You have not been doing your part that this gift be active through you. God is faithful, Timothy. He gave you the gift of the Holy Spirit. The Spirit remains in you. But mighty as He is in Himself, in you He is as but a tiny, tiny spark. He is alive in you, but through you He is affecting no one.

"Timothy, this gift in you has been given so that it might burn mightily within you. It has been given to shine brilliantly through you. It has been given to you so that the people you meet may be greatly impacted as it comes forth in power from you. Timothy, you are a vessel, chosen along with all other believers, to contain this great gift, this heavenly fire, as a source for its activity through you. You were not given this gift, the dynamic power of God Almighty, that it would remain within you, hidden quietly.

"Timothy, YOU have to fan into flame the Holy Spirit. Until now, you have kept Him as a glowing spark doing nothing.

"Timothy, this is a matter of using the principles of the sincere faith that I am sure is in you. By your faith, the anointing will flow forth from you to do all the things that the Lord Jesus gave to you to do. By faith, Timothy, as young as you are, a 'nobody' in ministry, the Holy

Spirit is in you to work wondrous things for the glory of the Anointed One, who gave the gift to you.

"Stop waiting for God to cause the Spirit to move through you. He has already acted on your behalf for the divine power to come from you. He gave you the gift. He gave you the measure of faith needed to stir up this flame. Now, do it. Put your sincere faith in the person of the Lord and in His words in John 7:37-39. Meditate on these words. Then act according to your faith in your daily life.

"Timothy, you have been given 'the gift of God,' His Spirit, not a spirit of timidity. Do not sit by, content with others ministering the anointing. It is timidity to live that way. Do not listen to the considerations of man in this matter. These are thoughts of false humility.

"Are you worthy to do such ministry, Timothy? Yes, you are young. Yes, you may appear unprepared in the eyes of some men. Of course, you are not worthy. But what man is worthy? Am I worthy? Of course not! But who does the Lord Jesus have to do such ministry if not those of us to whom He has given this gift. We may all be unworthy, but let us get on with doing what the Lord expects of us in this matter!

"Timothy, the ministry of the anointing is for ANYONE, young or old, unlearned or scholar, poor or rich, man or woman, titled or common. ANYONE who has the gift can minister that gift — by using his own faith — whenever he wants to.

"You have been given 'the gift of God,' the Spirit of divine power, the Spirit of love, the Spirit of self-discipline. God's power is ever available to you. The Spirit of love is with you to motivate you to bring to others the blessings the anointing affords. The Spirit is in you to enable you to discipline yourself. Lean on Him for this, that He animate you to minister Him continually.

"False humility, timidity, shame in the presence of others ... these are all enemies of the ministry of the gift. The Spirit of self-discipline will enable you to minister Him at any and all times. You can discipline yourself in the Holy Spirit to boldness and to continual activity in your ministry of the anointing."

In verse 7, Paul spoke of *"timidity."* Then, in verse 8, he spoke of a close relative — *"shame."* He exhorted against being ashamed to share with others the precious matters the Lord has revealed to us.

In verses 11 and 12, he asserts that he was not ashamed of the wonderful blessings of the Gospel. How strong was Paul's holy boast in Romans 1:16: *"I am not ashamed of the gospel of Christ [the Anointed One], for it is the power of God unto salvation to every one that believeth"* (KJV). Why does Paul write so strongly about the matter of shame when it comes to ministering the anointing? Could it be that he once knew what it was to feel such shame? Could it be that having experienced such shame himself he had learned to discipline himself against it, even as he was exhorting Timothy to do? Had this been an area of human weakness in Paul that later became one of strength through his abiding in Christ for that strength?

There are times when all of us feel shame in certain situations when an opportunity presents itself to share the words of the Gospel with others. This is true, as well, regarding opportunities to minister the anointing. In a church situation, we may have no problem sharing the things of God with others, but in our daily living situations, it is often different — in our workplace, in intellectual surroundings, with people of secular importance, with older people, among skeptics and scorners. In surroundings such as these, the prospect of sharing the simple truths of the Word of God, and even more, a claim that one may actually cause God to manifest Himself then and there, easily causes one to feel shame.

Shame, timidity, fear of rejection ... these are all enemies of ministry to the needs of others. Let us recognize that such weakness exists in us, and let us pray for holy boldness regularly. Let us lean on the Lord for boldness in situations where ministry is called for.

I confess my own weakness in this matter. Although I have ministered the anointing thousands of times, have seen the anointing work marvels and know that the anointing is from Almighty God Himself, yet, in certain given moments, I have felt ashamed of openly declaring and offering the anointing to others. Often, I have had to deal strongly with this enemy of the anointing. The cry of Romans 1:16 becomes mine, and the Spirit makes it my experience.

In verse 7, Paul spoke of the anointing that had been given to Timothy, and then in verse 8, he told Timothy to be bold regarding the sharing or imparting of this anointing to others. Then, in verse 9, he tells Timothy (and, of course, you and me — ANYONE who has this great grace) that it had been given to him through Christ Jesus, the Anointed One. It is the Lord Jesus who baptizes men and women with the Holy Spirit. This bestowing of the anointing, Paul shows, is because of the purposes of God for man, not because any of us is ever worthy to have this great grace.

In giving the anointing to a man, God purposes that the anointing be active through that man. Therefore, put aside all thoughts and feelings to the contrary. Understand this well: the Lord Jesus has purposed to do things in the earth through the anointing of the Holy Spirit. His means of doing this is by putting the anointing in a man. Then, that man is expected to cause the anointing to go forth from him to do the works of God.

In the context of these verses, Paul exhorts us to a holy life. He is not referring to moral holiness. He has been speaking of the purposes of God regarding the ministry of the anointing. A man or woman who has the anointing residing permanently within is called to be separated unto the purpose for which God has given that great grace. One will be holy in that he or she is given to the ministry of the anointing. It would be a mark of unholiness to live without ministry. That would amount to frustrating the purpose of God in your life, in the situations that confront you that call for the anointing to be ministered.

Finally, in 2 Timothy 2:1, Paul tells us to be strong regarding this great grace, the gift of the anointing. Christ, the Anointed One, has given you the gift of the Holy Spirit that He may work many wonders through you. He has given you the anointing of the same Holy Spirit He has. The activity of the anointing through you is to be a major factor in your life. You are to have a strong ministry of the anointing! You are to be vigorous in pursuit of the ministering of the anointing. Such ministry must come to be one of the most significant things in your life.

May we all heed exhortation. You have been anointed to do so. *Your River Must Flow!*

To contact the author for seminars, retreats and other speaking engagements, please use the following address:

Albert Gengenbach
12807 Thistle Blossom Way
Upper Marlboro, MD 20772

e-mail address: river73739@cs.com